EVERYDAY ◆ grain-free GOURMET

EVERYDAY ◆ grain-free GOURMET

JODI BAGER *and* **JENNY LASS**

BREAKFAST, LUNCH, *and* DINNER

whitecap

Edited by Ann-Marie Metten
Proofread by Marilyn Bittman
Original design by Diane Yee
Food Photography by Joseph Marranca
Food Styling by Julie Zambonelli
Typeset by Megan Stagg

Printed in China by 1010 Printing Asia Ltd.

The publisher acknowledges the financial support of the Government of Canada through the Canada Book Fund (CBF) and the Province of British Columbia through the Book Publishing Tax Credit.

Library and Archives Canada Cataloguing in Publication

Bager, Jodi

   Everyday grain-free gourmet : breakfast, lunch, and dinner / Jodi Bager and Jenny Lass.

Includes index.
ISBN 978-1-55285-918-6

   1. Carbohydrate intolerance–Diet therapy–Recipes.
2. Intestines–Diseases–Diet therapy–Recipes. I. Lass, Jenny II. Title.

RM237.86.L38 2008   641.5'6383   C2007-905494-3

DEDICATION

To my dear husband Steven and our children, Samuel and Theodore, who fill my life with joy. And to the late Elaine Gottschall, who lives on in this life she saved. —JB

To my parents, Diana and Harold, for their unending support; to Helen Leask and the entire SCRIPT office for providing me with space to think, write, and create; and to the late Elaine Gottschall and Dr. Sidney Haas for saving my life and so many others. —JL

TABLE OF CONTENTS

ACKNOWLEDGMENTS

As it happens, my immediate family is large and each member has been a part of this book as they sample new foods, offer constructive feedback, and even make recipe suggestions. My thanks go to my parents, Wendy and Elliott Eisen and Morton and Jill Litwack; my in-laws, Judith and Norman Bager; my sisters and brothers-in-law, Tammy and Paul Brown, Robin and Bill Sims, Jennifer and Bob Grossman, Kim and Tom Hansen, and Pamela Bager and Hart Mallin. My dearest friends, who are like family, Beverley and Peter Gold and Gillian and John Marshall, who saw me through the worst of my disease and have been an invaluable source of friendship, encouragement, support, and ideas—book-related and otherwise—for the past seven years. My friends, Anat and Illy Taiber and Lani Zigelstein, who have been unwavering in their support and interest in both my business and this book—and for this I am most grateful. Many thanks to my friend Lougie Ang who works so hard to make things easier for me. As with our first cookbook, *Grain-Free Gourmet: Delicious Recipes for Healthy Living*, I have to thank my friend Krista Thompson, who introduced me to the Specific Carbohydrate Diet and set me on the path to restored health that now appears to have become my life's work. And last, thank you to Jenny Lass, who helps to make our well-matched partnership seem effortless. —JB

I thank my parents, Harold Lass and Diana Papsin Lass, who continue to encourage and support me through thick and thin. Thanks once again to my friends and family, who are always willing to taste my experiments (and give me honest feedback) and accommodate my fussy stomach when we have meals together. Thanks to Dr. Helen Leask and Nancy Lazar for their patience and advice, and for providing me with an office to write in and a water cooler to chat around; thank you to all of the people at SCRIPT for their support, good humor, and ideas. Thank you to Beth Golden, Lanni Zinberg-Swartz, Dr. David Perkins, Dr. Helen Leask, and especially Dr. John Ashkenas for making sure my science was sound, and to Margaret Aliharan and Monica Dingle (the HealthSearch team) for finding me the most obscure articles. Thanks also go to Harold Lass and Diana Papsin Lass, Jane Macijauskas, Tanya Spiegelberg, and Ann Saunders for their valued feedback. Thank you to Judy Herod (née Gottschall) for helping me to tell the story of the Specific Carbohydrate Diet accurately. Thank you to Kala Solway, who introduced me to the Specific Carbohydrate Diet, and to Dr. Christina Fisher who has always supported me being on the SCD. Finally, I thank Jodi Bager, whose partnership is helping me to realize my dreams and carry on the Haas–Gottschall legacy. —JL

The list of people who need to be acknowledged for this book is long. At the top is our publisher Robert McCullough at Whitecap Books and the entire Whitecap team, including our editor Ann-Marie Metten. Thanks again to our favorite photographer Joseph Marranca and our wonderful food stylist Julie Zambonelli. Thank you also to Orest Hrycak and the folks at Nella Cucina in Toronto for providing us with the beautiful dishware used in our photographs, and thanks to Bruno's Fine Foods for their generous donation to our photo shoot. Most of all, we want to thank you, our readers, for your encouragement through emails and phone calls and who, by loving our first book, made us want to write *this* book just for you.

"This is for the new book" is our standard opening line when we serve something new at dinner parties; it is invariably met with excitement as other foodies like us get to evaluate a new dish and be a part of the creative cookbook process. Their kind compliments (well-deserving or not) are most appreciated, but perhaps more so is the creative debate that often ensues as we try to dissect what makes a dish *almost* perfect and how it can be altered to become so. We would like to thank the following people who helped to stimulate our creativity: Franco Agostino, Mitchel and Caroline Altman, Tracy Barber, Maurizio Barbieri, Mark Bittman, Elena Cardenas, Nancy Corcoran, Joel Daiter, Stephen Daiter, Fannie DeCaria, Eastern Connecticut Beekeepers Association, Chef Christopher Ennew, Carol Frilegh, Kimberly Gibson, Deanna Goldberg, Beth Golden, Chef Robyn Goorevitch, Joan Gottschall, Judy Herod, Adam Griff and Lesley Sandler Griff, Luiba Grossman, Jane Macijauskas, Adrienne O'Callaghan, Chef Christopher Palik, Patricia Raskin, Serena Pollack, Randy Rosen, Marla Singer, Ella Speakes, Tanya Spiegelberg, our friends in the Upper Canada Lower Bowel Society, and Carole and Bernie Zucker.

INTRODUCTION

When we approached Whitecap Books back in 2003 with the concept for our first book, *Grain-Free Gourmet: Delicious Recipes for Healthy Living*, we were touched by their leap of faith as they decided to be the first mainstream publishing company to put out a grain-free cookbook. In April 2006, much to our surprise and delight, Whitecap asked for a second book—armed with a mandate to push the boundaries of creativity and culinary indulgence, we set to work. A few months later, we had developed a set of recipes that we knew would rival those in our first book.

Coming up with the theme of this book was simple. After years of teaching cooking classes, being interviewed, and providing counseling, the most common questions still relate to mealtimes: *What do you have for breakfast? What do you have for lunch? What do you have for dinner?* Whether or not these questions are raised because people are curious or at a complete loss, we knew this was the topic that we had to tackle for our second foray into the culinary world.

In *Everyday Grain-Free Gourmet: Breakfast, Lunch, and Dinner*, we not only provide entire meal ideas, but are also more adventurous (think lactose-free, grain-free sandwich wraps, gnocchi, peanut butter truffles, and cappuccino dacquoise). We even demystify fat and provide information about the Specific Carbohydrate Diet (SCD) that we gathered from the original research archives of renowned New York pediatrician Dr. Sidney Haas from the 1920s to the 1960s. We have also added a list of our favorite tools that will make life in the kitchen easier, and we include conveniences that received high praise from our first book, such as a guide for storing food, suggested substitutions for people who don't follow the Specific Carbohydrate Diet, and a list of cheeses that are virtually lactose-free.

We hope that *Everyday Grain-Free Gourmet: Breakfast, Lunch, and Dinner* finds a prominent spot (next to our first book!) in your kitchen. –Jodi and Jenny

THE POWER AND POTENTIAL OF THE SPECIFIC CARBOHYDRATE DIET

In our first cookbook, *Grain-Free Gourmet: Delicious Recipes for Healthy Living*, we introduced readers to the delicious, nutritious, healing, and simple Specific Carbohydrate Diet (SCD)—a diet that has helped thousands of people world-wide reclaim their health in the face of digestive disorders such as celiac disease, Crohn's disease, ulcerative colitis, and irritable bowel syndrome. Because awareness is growing about this remarkable therapy, we wanted to give the SCD some context by outlining its history, supporting research, and relevance to the modern treatment of digestive and other diseases.

TREATING CELIAC DISEASE WITH THE SPECIFIC CARBOHYDRATE DIET

Although the SCD is now followed by people with all sorts of conditions, it was first developed in the 1920s to treat only celiac disease. In fact, for much of the first half of the 20th century, the SCD was widely accepted by the medical community as the gold standard treatment for celiacs. Then, in the 1950s, the results of a study that focused on gluten—a protein component of certain grains, such as wheat, rye, and barley—altered the course of celiac diet therapy and the SCD was replaced by the gluten-free diet. Yet the SCD remains relevant to today's celiacs and could be the key to offering new options to treatment-resistant patients, hastening recovery, improving nutrition, and easing food preparation—it could even point the way to a cure.

THE DAYS BEFORE GLUTEN-FREE

Celiac disease has probably existed for thousands of years and was first described as far back as the second century by the Greek physician Aretaeus of Cappadocia. But it was British physician Dr. Samuel Gee who standardized its diagnosis in 1888. His accounts of this condition in the *Saint Bartholomew's Hospital Reports* were frightening —he wrote in detail about how children with celiac disease were left permanently weak, stunted in growth, and sometimes suffered for months or years before dying. Gee was also the one who realized that changing what celiacs ate was the key to their recovery. His prescribed diet, which eliminated milk and starchy foods, inspired other physicians to start searching for the best celiac nutritional regimen.

This dietary "big break" came 20 years later when two young doctors expanded on the work of Dr. Emmett Holt, Director of Children's Medicine at Bellevue Hospital in New York, and Dr. Christian Herter at New York's Columbia University. Holt and Herter observed that their patients had high levels of abnormal bacteria in their stools and became sick when they ate carbohydrates—remarkably, they tolerated proteins well and fats moderately well. In the 1920s, Drs. Sidney Haas and John Howland joined Holt and Herter in their lab and finally applied these findings in a way that let people with celiac disease live normal, healthy lives.

> **FATS, PROTEINS, AND CARBOHYDRATES** are organic compounds that supply energy to the body. We need all three nutrients to stay healthy.

Howland began by eliminating the food group that seemed to make celiacs the sickest: carbohydrates. And it worked. Celiac patients who followed Howland's carbohydrate-free eating plan improved dramatically. But it was concerns over this diet's lack of nutrition that led Haas to try introducing simpler carbohydrates in the form of certain fruits and vegetables. This change made all the difference. Although

Haas's diet didn't include more complex carbohydrates, such as grains and starches, his patients thrived on the food he prescribed, which not only healed the digestive system, but was also extremely nutritious. Twenty-five years later, Haas had transformed the prognosis of celiac disease—a condition that once killed half of its victims—by successfully treating hundreds of children with his Specific Carbohydrate Diet (SCD) (see **THE ORIGINAL SPECIFIC CARBOHYDRATE DIET** on page 4).

Unlike celiacs of the past, almost all of Haas's SCD patients recovered fully and remained in good health. Astonishingly, over 98 percent of the 561 children tracked by Haas and his son Dr. Merrill P. Haas were either cured or felt significantly better after following the diet (see **OF THE 561 CHILDREN** on page 5). Even though this research is considered scientifically weak by today's standards because it didn't include clinical trials, it's hard to ignore such high cure rates in children with celiac disease. So what happened to this amazing diet?

FROM GRAIN-FREE TO GLUTEN-FREE

There's a reason that many people haven't heard of the Specific Carbohydrate Diet—it was replaced. Despite decades of curing children with the grain-free SCD, the gluten-free diet was proposed, tested, and accepted in less than five years. This transition started in 1950 when a Dutch doctoral student named Willem Dicke noticed that children with celiac disease improved after flour supplies were disrupted during the Second World War. Dicke hypothesized that gluten was making celiacs sick, and by 1952, the prestigious British journal the *Lancet* had published an article that introduced his gluten theory to the world. The paper outlined a handful of case studies that seemed to confirm that it was gluten—and only gluten—that triggered celiac symptoms.

Now, while Dicke's theory was a departure from SCD theory, it wasn't totally off the mark. Interestingly, it helped to partially explain the success of the SCD, which happens to be gluten-free. But the gluten theory rejected the well-established evidence showing that it's also important for people with celiac disease to avoid eating certain carbohydrates. This didn't seem to matter. The less restrictive gluten-free diet, which allowed rice and other gluten-free starchy foods prohibited on the SCD, started to become the first choice of doctors and patients.

As the gluten theory became increasingly popular, its limitations started to emerge—the most obvious was that, unlike the SCD, the gluten-free diet didn't cure children with celiac disease (see **OF THE 561 CHILDREN** on page 5). Even though the gluten-free diet controlled symptoms, celiacs who followed it could never go back to eating an unrestricted diet without getting sick. Haas expressed his frustration over this in a 1963 *New York State Journal of Medicine* article: "[Gluten] is only one of the causes of the

THE ORIGINAL SPECIFIC CARBOHYDRATE DIET
developed by Dr. Sidney Haas was a little different from the one that is practiced today. Research conducted by Canadian food scientist Elaine Gottschall and published in *Breaking the Vicious Cycle: Intestinal Health Through Diet* led to slight changes in food choices, as shown in the following chart.

1960s SCD	Modern SCD
PROTEINS	
· all meats	· all unprocessed meats
· all fish, including canned, fresh, and shellfish	· processed meats are only allowed if the manufacturer can guarantee no additives, such as lactose, starch, gluten, refined sugars, or wheat
· unsweetened gelatin	· unsweetened gelatin
· all cheese, except processed	· all fish, including canned, fresh, and shellfish
· homemade yogurt fermented for 24 hours	· only aged, unprocessed cheeses and dry-curd cottage cheese
· eggs in any form, sparingly	· homemade yogurt fermented for 24 hours
	· eggs in any form
	· all nuts except salted nuts and shelled peanuts, which can have added starch
FATS	
· all fats, including oils and sour cream	· most fats, including butter and most oils
FLUID MILK	
· protein milk (milk that is whey-free) or its equivalent	· none
CARBOHYDRATES	
· all fresh fruits and all vegetables except potatoes and corn	· all fresh, frozen, or dried fruits
· honey, dates, raisins, and unsweetened fruit juices are allowed in amounts depending on the frequency and consistency of the stool	· fruit canned in its own juice with no added sugar
· no grains or refined sugar	· all fresh or frozen vegetables except potatoes, sweet potatoes, turnips, Jerusalem artichokes, and seaweed
	· honey, dates, raisins, and unsweetened fruit juices are allowed in amounts depending on the frequency and consistency of the stool
	· no refined sugar or grains, including corn
	· no soybeans, chickpeas, bean sprouts, fava beans, garbanzo beans, or mung beans
	· no cocoa, not even cocoa powder or unsweetened, dairy-free chocolate

celiac syndrome, and although great improvement follows its omission from the diet, only a partial cure results, since most cases relapse if gluten is eaten."

The gluten-free diet had another big problem. Some people with celiac disease didn't respond to it at all. Although the small number of children who were documented in the 1952 *Lancet* article improved when they stopped eating gluten, later studies showed that some celiacs were "refractory"—in other words, they continued to get sick despite following a gluten-free diet. Researchers found that many seemingly refractory patients eventually got better after eliminating hidden sources of gluten in their food. However, a study conducted by doctors at the Mayo Clinic and published in 2002 in the *American Journal of Gastroenterology* revealed that 18 percent of their refractory celiac study participants were completely unresponsive to the gluten-free diet.

The development of the gluten theory also brought with it a new, yet flawed, way to diagnose celiac disease: the intestinal biopsy. This test involves taking a tissue sample from the intestinal wall to look for damaged villi—finger-like projections on the surface of the small intestine that help absorb nutrients. Although abnormal villi can be a symptom of many conditions, such as hepatitis and ulcerative colitis, the medical community insisted that an intestinal biopsy was one of the best ways to identify "true celiacs." Patients who had normal

OF THE 561 CHILDREN reported on in the *American Journal of Gastroenterology* and *Postgraduate Medicine* by Drs. Sidney and Merrill Haas—

· **463 (82.5 percent) were cured* after following the SCD and were able to return to a normal diet**

   · 190 within 18 months
   · 271 within 3 years
   · One within 4.5 years
   · One within 6 years

· **89 (16 percent) had just started the SCD, but their symptoms were under control and they seemed to be on the road to recovery**

· **Six were not cured**

   · Five refused to follow the SCD strictly
   · One had a relapse following an asthma attack

· **Three died from causes unrelated to celiac disease**

* The Drs. Haas defined a cured child as one "who shows excellent nutrition, an adequate and happy personality, complete absence of stool abnormality without even temporary diarrhea over short periods, and who can eat a completely unrestricted diet without any recurrence of symptoms." Haas and his son also noted that celiacs who started the SCD as adults couldn't be cured, but they stayed symptom-free as long as they continued to follow the diet.

biopsy results, but who still met Haas's diagnostic criteria ("a history of prolonged intermittent soft-loose, frequent, foul, and mucus-laden stools"), were either misdiagnosed or remained undiagnosed and untreated.

In spite of the gluten theory's diagnostic and treatment shortcomings, Haas lost his fight for acceptance of the SCD in a post gluten theory world, and his diet vanished from mainstream medical doctrine after his death in 1964. The definition and diagnosis of celiac disease continued to evolve to fit the gluten theory with the development of diagnostic blood tests in the 1970s, '80s, and '90s that only measured the effect of gluten on the body (and to this day sometimes yield false results). Celiac disease is currently defined as an autoimmune response in the intestines triggered by eating gluten, and as would be expected, today most people with celiac disease follow the gluten-free diet.

AN AUTOIMMUNE RESPONSE is the attack on a person's tissues by his or her own immune system. A celiac's immune system attacks the lining of the intestines in the same way that the immune system of someone with rheumatoid arthritis attacks the joints.

TODAY'S CELIACS AND THE SPECIFIC CARBOHYDRATE DIET

The SCD hasn't been completely forgotten by the celiac community—a number of people with celiac disease have discovered the benefits of the SCD and choose it over the gluten-free diet. One reason celiacs sometimes prefer the SCD is that, in many ways, it's easier to follow, despite its tighter restrictions. For example, the SCD's almond-flour baked goods are simple to make and authentic tasting, while standard gluten-free baking recipes can involve long lists of hard-to-find ingredients and produce baked goods that don't always measure up in terms of taste and texture. The SCD is also extremely nutritious because it is a whole foods diet, unlike the gluten-free diet, which allows many processed, less nutritious foods that are loaded with preservatives, fillers, and refined sugars.

In addition, people with both celiac disease and diabetes are becoming interested in the SCD because it lets them simultaneously meet the dietary requirements of these two conditions—the SCD not only heals the intestines, but can also help control insulin levels thanks to its low-carb nut-based baked goods.

Not surprisingly, celiacs who are refractory or don't respond quickly to the gluten-free diet are also drawn to the SCD and can find it to be highly effective (see **JENNY'S STORY** on page 7). Canadian food scientist Elaine Gottschall, who studied the SCD after Haas's death, was finally able to provide more information about why a mostly complex-carb-free diet seemed to work better than a diet that only eliminated gluten—her research not only confirmed the observations made back in 1908 by Holt and Herter (see page 2), but also identified the biochemical reasons the SCD was so successful.

According to Gottschall, the damaged celiac gut can't digest certain carbohydrates, such as grains, starches, and some sugars (including lactose). These undigested carbohydrates ferment in the intestines, causing the harmful accumulation of "bad" bacteria (bacterial overgrowth)—this bacteria leads to more intestinal damage and diarrhea. By eliminating harder-to-digest carbohydrates, the SCD deprives "bad" bacteria of their fuel and allows damaged intestines to heal. More recent research presented in a 2003 volume of the *American Journal of Gastroenterology* further supports this theory by documenting intestinal bacterial overgrowth and lactose intolerance in many celiacs who don't respond quickly to the gluten-free diet.

It is essential to continue studying the SCD in the context of modern science, not only so the sickest celiacs can get well, but also to revisit the diet's reported ability to cure children with celiac disease. There is clearly a powerful healing mechanism involved in the SCD that needs to be investigated further by researchers. Fortunately, hope exists for formal SCD studies because modern physicians are beginning to notice the diet's positive effect on other conditions, such as Crohn's disease, ulcerative colitis, irritable bowel syndrome, and autism spectrum disorder.

TREATING OTHER CONDITIONS WITH THE SPECIFIC CARBOHYDRATE DIET

One of the most well-known SCD success stories is that of Elaine and Herbert Gottschall's daughter, Judy. In the 1950s, the Gottschalls were living in New Jersey when Judy developed severe ulcerative colitis at the age of four. When conventional treatments failed, doctors threatened to remove Judy's colon. Elaine and Herbert began a desperate search for another opinion and went from doctor to doctor, with no luck. Just when they were about to give up, they were referred to Dr. Sidney Valentine Haas—developer of the SCD. Judy started following the SCD and felt better within two weeks. Within two years, she was symptom-free. She remains in remission and on an unrestricted diet to this day.

Elaine went back to school at age 47 to continue where Haas left off in his research. She earned degrees in biology, nutritional biochemistry, and cellular biology from institutions in New Jersey and Ontario, Canada, finally graduating with a master's degree in science from the University of Western Ontario in 1979. Several years later, Elaine wrote *Food and the Gut Reaction* (Kirkton Press, 1987), an SCD resource for the lay reader, which was eventually renamed *Breaking the Vicious Cycle: Intestinal Health Through Diet* (Kirkton Press, 1994). In this book, she describes the history of the diet and the science supporting it. She also provides the first official set of SCD recipes and instructions on key SCD techniques, such as almond-flour baking and lactose-free yogurt making, which we feature in this cookbook and in our first cookbook, *Grain-Free Gourmet: Delicious Recipes for Healthy Living*. Elaine died in September 2005 in Grafton, Ontario, but *Breaking the Vicious Cycle* is still in print and has sold over one million copies worldwide.

Elaine's daughter isn't the only person with an inflammatory bowel disease whose life was changed by the SCD (see **JODI'S STORY** on page 9). As with celiac disease, no strong studies or clinical trials have been done to test how or why the SCD helps people with Crohn's disease and ulcerative colitis, but physician case studies and hundreds of testimonials suggest that this diet works wonders. It appears that the SCD can control inflammatory bowel disease symptoms, allow conventional treatments to work better, and work when traditional treatments fail. There are even other stories like Judy's (see above) that document the SCD's ability to send some inflammatory bowel disease patients into remission.

Two of these incredible accounts can be found in a 2004 *Tennessee Medicine* article by Drs. Raquel Nieves and Roger Jackson. These doctors describe two women with inflammatory bowel diseases who were becoming desperate after developing a resistance to steroid treatment. Both patients turned to the SCD and felt better within a matter of days. Within a month, they were off all medication and soon tice, these doctors encountered two children with Crohn's disease whose health was restored thanks to the diet. The first patient was an 11-year-old girl who was symptom-free with normal test results after six months on the SCD, and the second was a nine-year-old boy who was symptom-free with normal test results after only three months on the diet. Both children were off all medication. The article called for more research on the SCD and, in particular, its apparent gift for healing by controlling intestinal bacteria.

The doctors at Stanford are just a few of the many health professionals who have been taking an interest in the link between intestinal bacteria and inflammatory bowel diseases. A study in the October 2007 issue of the journal *Cell* has even found another factor that may contribute to bacterial overgrowth in people with ulcerative colitis: a deficiency in a protein called T-bet. This T-bet shortage leads to an immune response that leaves the intestinal wall vulnerable to attack by "bad" bacteria.

As a result of the growing awareness of the relationship between bacteria and intestinal conditions, more and more researchers are starting to investigate the possibility of treating not only inflammatory bowel diseases, but also irritable bowel syndrome (see **CROHN'S DISEASE AND ULCERATIVE COLITIS** on page 10) with probiotics, or "good" bacteria that keep the many harmful bacteria in the intestines in check. The SCD actually uses the healing

after, achieved remission. Nieves and Jackson also talk about the results of an Internet survey they conducted on 51 people with inflammatory bowel diseases who followed the SCD. Of those surveyed, 84 percent had achieved remission and 61 percent were off all medication.

Physicians at the Stanford Medical Center tell two more SCD success stories in a 2004 paper published in the *Journal of Pediatric Gastroenterology and Nutrition*. In their practice, power of probiotics through homemade lactose-free yogurt whose probiotic content is boosted by its long fermentation time (at least 24 hours).

Research published in a 2005 issue of the *American Journal of Gastroenterology* confirms that probiotics can play a key role in treating people with inflammatory bowel diseases. This article outlines a clinical trial of probiotics on people with ulcerative colitis who didn't respond to drug therapy. Of the 34 patients in the study, 53 percent reached remission and 24 percent improved—none experienced side effects from the treatment. Another *American Journal of Gastroenterology* article published in 2006 reports that a significant number of study participants with irritable bowel syndrome finally found relief from abdominal pain, bloating, bowel dysfunction, constipation, and gas when they took a probiotic called *Bifidobacterium infantis* 35624.

Even though there are fewer "good" bacteria in SCD yogurt than in probiotic supplements, the results of these studies strongly support SCD theory, which emphasizes how important it is to control bacterial overgrowth in the intestines when treating digestive disorders.

Another group that is exploring the healing potential of the SCD is parents of children diagnosed with autism spectrum disorder (ASD). ASD is a brain disorder that develops in childhood that affects behavior, social interaction, and communication. One in 150 North Americans has ASD and many of them suffer simultaneously from digestive diseases, making their care even more challenging.

Some caregivers have noticed changes in the behavior and communication patterns of children with ASD after their diet is altered to relieve digestive symptoms—some call this phenomenon the brain-gut connection. Even though the medical community has noted similar links between intestinal dysfunction and brain dysfunction throughout history, researchers have only recently begun to conduct studies to find out whether or not there is a scientific basis for this observation.

Within the past several years, a number of caregivers have started trying to harness the brain-gut connection through diet to control behavioral and communication ASD symptoms. There has been a lot in the news about the gluten-free, casein-free (GFCF) diet, which is one food-based therapy that parents sometimes use along with their child's traditional ASD intervention program. But the results of the first double-blind, controlled trial on the GFCF diet published in March 2006 in the *Journal of Autism and Developmental Disorders* showed no significant improvement in the small sample of children studied. Some parents who have found that their children don't improve on the GFCF diet have turned to the Specific Carbohydrate Diet and have achieved positive results. Formal Specific Carbohydrate Diet–based autism treatment programs are now available at The Gottschall Autism Center in Massachusetts.

However, the mainstream medical community doesn't support using the GFCF diet or the Specific Carbohydrate Diet to treat ASD because their effectiveness hasn't been proved in clinical trials. Formal research on these diets must continue so both physicians and parents have clear answers.

WHERE ARE WE NOW?

This is an exciting time in medicine. The connections between health and diet are becoming stronger as research in this area grows. Before long, the SCD and other diet therapies will begin to play more prominent roles in mainstream medical practice, offering patients more treatment options with fewer side effects.

SPECIFIC CARBOHYDRATE DIET TIMELINE

ROMAN EMPIRE	Aretaeus first describes celiac disease.
1888	Dr. Gee establishes criteria for diagnosing celiac disease.
1908	Drs. Holt and Herter note that celiacs have abnormal bacteria in their stools and a low tolerance for carbohydrates.
1921	Dr. Howland treats celiacs with a carbohydrate-free diet.
1924	Dr. Haas identifies carbohydrates that celiacs can digest.
1951	Dr. Haas and his son outline the Specific Carbohydrate Diet in the medical textbook *The Management of Celiac Disease*.
1952	A small study concludes that gluten triggers intestinal damage in celiacs—the gluten-free diet gains instant acceptance.
1955	Judy Gottschall is diagnosed with severe ulcerative colitis.
1958	Dr. Haas puts Judy on the SCD.
1960	Judy is cured.
1964	Dr. Haas dies.
1973	Judy's mother Elaine Gottschall goes back to school to continue researching the SCD.
1987	Elaine Gottschall introduces the general public to the SCD in her book *Food and the Gut Reaction*, which is later republished as *Breaking the Vicious Cycle: Intestinal Health Through Diet*.
2005	Elaine Gottschall dies.
TODAY	*Breaking the Vicious Cycle: Intestinal Health Through Diet* has sold over one million copies and has been translated into seven languages.

FATS—THE GOOD, THE BAD, AND THE NOT-AS-BAD-AS-YOU-THINK

In our first cookbook, *Grain-Free Gourmet: Delicious Recipes for Healthy Living*, we debunked the egg–cholesterol myth; now we would like to clear up a few misconceptions about fat. North America has become a hotbed of fat phobia. We have invented low-fat everything and created ways to eat fat without absorbing it—remember Olestra, the food additive that made unhealthy snacks low-fat but caused cramps and diarrhea? We have even marketed products that never contained fat in the first place as "fat-free." It's no wonder some of our readers question our use of high-fat almonds and dairy. While it's true that many people need to reduce their fat intake, fat isn't all bad—in fact, fat is necessary.

WHAT IS FAT?

Fat is one of the three nutrients that supplies energy to the body. It provides nine calories per gram, which is twice as much provided by each of the two other nutrients: carbohydrates and protein.

WHY DO WE NEED FAT?

Although most of us spend our time trying to avoid fat, it's an essential part of a healthy diet. Aside from helping you feel full longer, fat helps your body make hormones; gives you long-lasting energy; contributes to the formation of your brain and nervous system; creates cell membranes; carries the fat-soluble vitamins A, D, E, and K throughout your body; regulates body temperature; and helps to maintain healthy hair and skin.

US dietary guidelines (see **RESOURCES** on page 212) recommend keeping total fat intake between 20 and 35 percent of your daily calories. Canadian dietary guidelines advise incorporating 2 to 3 Tbsp (30 to 45 mL) of unsaturated fat (see **GOOD FAT** below) into your diet each day and keeping total fat intake to 30 percent or less of your daily calories. No more than 10 percent of your daily calories should come from saturated fat (see **BAD FAT** on page 16).

TYPES OF FAT
GOOD FAT

Fat is classified as "good" if it helps decrease your risk of developing heart disease by lowering blood LDL levels (the "bad" cholesterol) and raising blood HDL levels (the "good" cholesterol). The "good" fats include monounsaturated and polyunsaturated fats, known collectively as unsaturated fats. That's why

OTHER SOURCES OF "GOOD" FAT INCLUDE:

- fatty fish, such as mackerel and salmon
- olives
- olive, corn, safflower, sunflower, soybean, cottonseed, canola, and peanut oils
- most nuts
- avocados

many of our baked goods include almond flour, which is high in not only unsaturated fats, but also fiber, vitamins, and minerals.

However, the unsaturated fat in almonds does more than just lower LDL. According to a 2003 article in the *International Journal of Obesity and Related Metabolic Disorders*, an almond-enriched, low-calorie diet high in monounsaturated fats can help people who are overweight lose more weight than a low-calorie diet high in complex carbohydrates. After six months, study participants on the almond diet had a 62 percent greater reduction in their weight and body mass index, a 50 percent greater reduction in waist circumference, and a 56 percent greater reduction in body fat than those on the low-calorie, high-carbohydrate diet. Researchers guess certain kinds of fish, is beneficial to the brain. DHA may contribute to increased intelligence and better vision in children and can help treat neurological illnesses, such as Alzheimer's disease in its early stages and depression. Recipes in this book that contain fish rich in DHA include **DRY-RUB SALMON BARBECUED ON A CEDAR PLANK** (page 142), **SEARED TUNA WITH CARROT FRITTERS** (page 145), **PORTUGUESE BACALHAU (SALT COD)** (page 140), and **SPICY PEEL-AND-EAT SHRIMP** (page 143). If you don't like fish, fish oil supplements are a good alternative. If you are allergic to fish, there are foods with added DHA, such as omega-3 eggs and omega-3 yogurt, but they don't contain nearly as much DHA as fish or supplements.

BAD FAT

There are two basic "bad" fats. The first is trans fat, which has gained a reputation as the worst fat you can eat. Studies show that trans fats increase your risk of developing heart disease by not only raising LDL (the "bad" cholesterol), but also lowering HDL (the "good" cholesterol). Special labeling is required for packaged foods containing trans fats and in 2007, New York became the first North American city to ban trans fats in restaurants. Although trans fats are found in small amounts in natural whole foods, such as dairy products, beef, and lamb, they are mainly found in large amounts in many

ALMONDS WERE NOT ALWAYS SO PROMINENT IN THE SPECIFIC CARBOHYDRATE DIET. While nuts were allowed on the original diet (see **THE ORIGINAL SPECIFIC CARBOHYDRATE DIET** on page 4), it was Elaine Gottschall who introduced the European tradition of baking with nut flour when she revived the diet in the 1980s. Almond was Elaine's flour of choice because of its high nutritional value, and its mild, neutral flavor, which makes it perfect for baking everything from savory to sweet treats. Some of the recipes in this cookbook that feature nutritious, delicious almond flour include **WAFFLES AND PANCAKES** (page 61), **SUN-DRIED TOMATO AND BASIL CRACKERS** (page 97), **GOURMET PIZZA WITH POACHED PEAR, CARAMELIZED ONION, AND GORGONZOLA CHEESE** (page 108), **OPEN-FACED CHICKEN POT PIE** (page 148), **CRISPY SOUTHERN CHICKEN** (page 151), **APPLE CAKE** (page 173), and **GINGER COOKIES** (page 186).

that this strategy—eating fat to lose fat—may work because unsaturated fats help you feel full longer and can prevent unhealthy snacking high in empty calories and "bad" fats (see **BAD FAT** on this page).

Evidence also suggests that docosahexaenoic acid (DHA), one of the "good" fats found in processed foods. Always read the nutritional information on labels before buying packaged foods to make sure you are getting as little trans fat as possible. In ingredient lists, look for key words such as "hydrogenated" and "partially hydrogenated." Manufacturers that use these terms have turned liquid oil into a more solid state with chemical processes called hydrogenation and partial hydrogenation that actually create trans fats.

The other "bad" fat is saturated fat. Saturated fat isn't considered as harmful as trans fat because it increases both LDL and HDL levels—the "bad" and the "good" cholesterols. Plus, not all saturated fats are created equal. Coconuts are extremely high in saturated fat, but have been prominent in the diets of healthy tropical populations for centuries. Scientists believe that this is likely because most of the saturated fat in unprocessed coconut is made up of medium chain fatty acids whose properties are different from the saturated fat found in animal products.

However, that doesn't mean that animal products are bad for you just because they contain saturated fat—in fact, some contain less saturated fat than you might think. Over 50 percent of the fat in beef is unsaturated and about 30 percent of the saturated fat in beef is stearic acid, which is healthier than other saturated fats because, like the saturated fat in coconut, it metabolizes differently. Only about 3 percent of the fat in beef is trans fat.

ANIMAL PRODUCTS THAT CONTAIN SATURATED FAT:

- beef and veal
- chicken
- lamb
- pork
- dairy
- eggs

Just remember to keep your total intake of saturated fat to 10 percent or less of your daily calories. It's easy to meet this goal by eating lean meats and low-fat dairy products, which allow you to benefit from the excellent nutrition found in them without overindulging in saturated fat. For example, beef is rich in protein, iron, B vitamins, and zinc, and dairy is an excellent source of calcium and vitamin D, which can help to prevent osteoporosis or brittle bones.

Studies also indicate that despite dairy's fat content, it can help in the maintenance of a healthy weight. Randomized clinical trials have shown that adults who are obese lose significantly more weight and/or body fat on a diet that includes three servings of milk, yogurt, or cheese a day. A 2004 article in *Obesity Research* reported that obese adults on a low-calorie, high-dairy diet lost 70 percent

BUTTER VERSUS MARGARINE—it's a long-standing debate. Which is healthier? Each has benefits and drawbacks. Despite its saturated fat content and potentially small amount of lactose, butter is the choice of people following the SCD because it has no preservatives or additives and contains 16 trace nutrients, including vitamins A and D and the minerals calcium and iron. The calories in butter are about equal to those in traditional margarine spreads, so, if eaten in moderation, butter can be part of a healthy diet. People following the SCD who are sensitive to lactose can remove it from butter through a process called clarification (see **CLARIFIED BUTTER** on page 33). Margarine is usually the choice of people with heart disease because most brands don't contain saturated or trans fats. However, some margarines are high in trans fats, so be sure to read labels carefully. All margarines contain artificial colors and flavors, and even though margarine has some nutritional value, it does not compare to that of butter.

THE BOTTOM LINE

Remember that fat is an important part of a healthy diet, but should be eaten in moderation. Following the SCD is an excellent way to source the fat you need in the form of natural whole foods.

more body weight and 64 percent more body fat than those on a low-dairy diet. Researchers hypothesize that the natural calcium found in dairy (as opposed to calcium found in supplements) plays a crucial role in the body's system for regulating fat and weight.

KITCHEN BASICS

HOW TO STORE YOUR FOOD

In our first cookbook, *Grain-Free Gourmet: Delicious Recipes for Healthy Living,* we provided a food storage guide to take the guesswork out of eating leftovers. Our readers loved this tool, so once again, here are some tips for storing foods from our recipes safely. Follow these storage guidelines unless otherwise specified in the recipe and always refrigerate or freeze leftovers within 2 hours of cooking.

FOOD ITEM	At Room Temperature	In the Refrigerator 4°C (40°F) or Colder	In the Freezer −18°C (0°F) or Colder
BEEF, POULTRY, AND FISH			
cooked meat and meat dishes (e.g., baked chicken)	—	3 to 4 days	2 to 3 months
gravy and meat broth (chicken stock)	—	1 to 2 days	2 to 3 months
casseroles	—	1 to 2 days	2 to 3 months
leftover meat dishes with sauce	—	1 to 2 days	6 months
burgers	—	1 to 2 days	1 to 3 months
chopped liver	—	3 to 4 days	1 month
cooked fish and seafood	—	1 to 2 days	1 to 3 months
tuna salad	—	3 to 4 days	—
DAIRY PRODUCTS			
milk	—	5 days past carton date	1 month (freezing affects flavor and appearance)
butter	—	3 weeks	3 months (unsalted) 1 year (salted)

FOOD ITEM	At Room Temperature	In the Refrigerator 4°C (40°F) or Colder	In the Freezer −18°C (0°F) or Colder
hard cheeses	—	6 months unopened, 3 to 4 weeks opened	6 months
yogurt	—	10 days	—
yogurt cheese and cream cheese	—	10 days	—
ice cream	—	—	2 to 3 months
EGGS			
fresh, in shell	—	3 to 5 weeks	—
raw yolks, whites	—	2 to 4 days	1 year separated yolks and whites, 6 months beaten whole egg
scrambled	—	1 to 2 days	—
omelets	—	2 to 3 days	—
hard-boiled	—	1 week	1 year
liquid pasteurized eggs, opened	—	3 days	1 year
liquid pasteurized eggs, unopened	—	10 days	2 to 3 months
crêpes	—	2 to 3 days	2 to 3 months
quiche	—	2 to 3 days	—
egg salad	—	3 to 4 days	—

FOOD ITEM	At Room Temperature	In the Refrigerator 4°C (40°F) or Colder	In the Freezer –18°C (0°F) or Colder
homemade mayonnaise and aioli	—	2 to 3 weeks	—
ALMOND-FLOUR BAKED GOODS			
muffins, cakes, waffles, pancakes, and breads	2 days	1 week	2 to 3 months
pies	1 to 2 days	4 days	2 to 3 months
pizza	—	4 days	2 to 3 months
tiramisu	—	1 week	—
crackers in an airtight container	2 months	—	3 months
cookies	1 week	2 weeks	2 to 3 months
FRUIT DESSERTS	—	2 to 3 days	—
CANDY	—	1 to 2 weeks	2 to 3 months
JAMS AND MARMALADES	—	2 months	6 months
SAUCES AND SOUPS			
without meat	—	5 to 7 days	2 to 3 months
with meat	—	1 to 2 days	2 to 3 months
APPETIZERS AND SIDE DISHES	—	2 to 4 days	2 to 3 months
SALAD DRESSINGS	—	1 week to 10 days	—
SALADS (tuna, chicken, egg, salmon)	—	3 to 4 days	—

KITCHEN TOOLS THAT WILL MAKE YOUR LIFE EASIER

Everyone has their favorite kitchen gadgets. Here are some of our favorites that we've found make life a whole lot easier.

8-INCH (20-CM) NONSTICK OMELET PAN: As far as we are concerned, a small nonstick omelet pan is an essential kitchen tool. It's perfect for frying eggs, cooking small amounts of onion and garlic, pancakes, crêpes, and, of course, omelets. Invest in a good, heavy one and it will serve you well!

COFFEE GRINDER: You might have one coffee grinder, but do you have two? Use one as it was intended—for coffee beans; use the second for grinding herbs and whole spices.

CRÊPE MAKER: Okay, it's not as authentic, but a crêpe maker helps you easily make perfect, delicious crêpes at home.

FOOD PROCESSOR: Without a doubt, a food processor is one of the greatest kitchen tools. It's perfect for grating cheese, slicing vegetables, puréeing large batches of soup, and even making mayonnaise. For simplifying many jobs in the kitchen, the food processor is it!

HANDHELD OR IMMERSION BLENDER: Use a handheld or immersion blender to save time and reduce mess by puréeing soups or sauces right in the pot.

PARCHMENT PAPER: We use parchment paper a lot. We don't enjoy wrestling with baked goods when prying them from their pan and we're sure you don't either. So our advice is, when in doubt, use parchment paper. We have found that it provides the most effective nonstick surface.

PORTABLE TIMER: Have you ever left your kitchen and forgotten that you had something in the oven? If you have, a portable timer is for you. Carry it with you (some even clip onto your clothes) so that in the middle of multi-tasking you won't forget that you need to get back in the kitchen to take your muffins out of the oven.

RASP ZESTER: A stainless-steel rasp is an easy way to zest oranges, lemons, and other citrus fruit. The rasp removes just the fine layer of zest that contains the essential oils and flavor of the fruit—without the bitter white pith. Find a rasp zester at a kitchen store or use a fine rasp from a woodworking store.

SQUEEZE BOTTLE: A plastic squeeze bottle similar to the kind used to serve ketchup at a delicatessen is great for dribbling oil slowly when making mayonnaise so the oil emulsifies and the ingredients don't separate.

STANDING BLENDER: Great for making smoothies, a standing blender is also helpful for puréeing vegetables before they are added to soups. A standing blender has fewer parts to clean than a food processor, making cleanup quick and easy.

VEGETABLE STEAMER: This little inexpensive gadget resembles a metal basket with holes. It allows steam to cook vegetables thereby preserving nutrients that can otherwise be lost in the water when vegetables are boiled.

WAFFLE IRON: If you want a break from pancakes, waffles are a good alternative. Waffle irons come in more shapes and sizes than you can imagine—round, heart-shaped, Belgian-sized, stick-shaped. You can even buy one in the shape of Mickey Mouse's face! A waffle iron is a great tool to help easily jazz up your breakfast.

WATER-RESISTANT OVEN MITTS: Do you always seem to be fighting with heavy, wet, stained oven mitts? If so, water-resistant oven mitts are for you. They rinse clean in seconds and dry quickly. Most importantly, your hands will stay dry no matter how dirty your mitts get.

STANDARDS

In this section you will find standard recipes for crêpes, jams, sauces, syrups, nut mixes, and yogurts—staples that you will need as ingredients for some of the other dishes in this book. Many of these recipes became popular in our cooking classes, or are frequently requested, such as **PURE VANILLA EXTRACT** (page 36). Most of these recipes are new, but a few of them appeared in our first book. The reason for this repetition is simple: we would like everyone who buys our first cookbook, *Grain-Free Gourmet: Delicious Recipes for Healthy Living*, to do so because they want to, not because they need its mayonnaise recipe to make the sandwich wrap recipe in this book! So forgive us if you have seen some of these recipes before. We promise that you won't be disappointed with the variety in this section or in the rest of the book.

YOGURT

Makes 8 cups (2 L)

If you follow the Specific Carbohydrate Diet, you probably know that homemade yogurt can be the magic bullet to getting better when you have intestinal problems. Making your own yogurt as outlined in this recipe will produce not only the best yogurt you likely ever tasted, but also a far greater number of good bacteria because it is fermented longer than regular store-bought yogurt. The method you follow here is the same whether you use skim, 1%, 2%, or whole (3.5%) milk or half-and-half (10%) or whipping cream (35%). Remember, if you are making yogurt with half-and-half or whipping cream, you must use organic products because conventional creams contain additives that can irritate sensitive stomachs.

1. Bring the milk or cream to a boil and immediately remove it from the stove.

2. Cool it to room temperature or colder. You can refrigerate the milk or cream to speed the process.

3. If you are using plain yogurt as your starter, pour 1 cup (250 mL) of the prepared milk or cream into a clean bowl, add the yogurt, and mix well. Alternatively, if you are using powdered yogurt starter, pour 2 packages (10 mL) of starter into a bowl and add 1 cup (250 mL) of the prepared milk or cream. Mix well.

4. Add the starter mixture to the rest of the prepared milk or cream and combine well.

5. Pour into a yogurt maker and follow the manufacturer's instructions, **but not for the suggested fermentation time**.

6. Plug in the yogurt maker and **let the yogurt ferment for 24 to 30 hours**. Most people find that 24 hours is enough.

7. Refrigerate the yogurt for 6 to 8 hours to allow it to firm and thicken.

8. Store in the refrigerator for up to 10 days.

8 cups (2 L) **pasteurized milk** or **organic cream**

½ cup (125 mL) **plain store-bought yogurt** or 2 packages (10 mL) **powdered yogurt starter**

YOGURT CHEESE

Makes 1½ to 2 cups (375 to 500 mL)

Yogurt cheese is an invaluable staple in our kitchens. It adds a creamy texture to **SWEET SQUASH KUGEL** (page 125) or the filling for **OPEN-FACED CHICKEN POT PIE** (page 148). Sprinkle in a bit of salt and it becomes cream cheese (see below), or use it in desserts, such as **GRILLED PEACHES WITH SWEETENED YOGURT CHEESE** (page 169) and **TIRA-MISU** (page 181). Feel free to use store-bought yogurt to make yogurt cheese if you don't follow the Specific Carbohydrate Diet.

4 cups (1 L) **homemade YOGURT** (page 27) or **plain store-bought yogurt**

1. Soak the cotton bag that comes with your yogurt maker in boiling water for about 1 minute. Spoon the yogurt into the bag and hang it at room temperature on a cupboard handle or nail. The yogurt will start dripping as soon as it's in the bag, so make sure a container is under it. Alternatively, you can drip yogurt in a colander or sieve lined with cheesecloth.

2. Let drip for 6 to 8 hours. Remove the cheese from the dripping device and store it in the refrigerator.

CREAM CHEESE

Yogurt cheese can be easily turned into cream cheese by adding a little salt to taste. Use yogurt cheese to get the rich texture of cream cheese with the healthy dose of the good bacteria that comes from yogurt.

GOAT'S MILK YOGURT

Makes 8 cups (2 L)

Some people simply cannot digest yogurt made from cow's milk. Goat's milk is sometimes more easily digested by people who are sensitive to dairy because it contains a different kind of protein and 13 percent less lactose than cow's milk, so feel free to use this recipe as a substitute in some of our dishes that call for cow's milk yogurt. Note that the goat's milk yogurt has a strong taste and won't work well in sweet dishes, such as the **LEMON FREEZE** (page 175) or **TIRAMISU** (page 181). However, goat's milk yogurt will taste great in the **FRITTATA** (page 66) and most other savory meals. This recipe will also allow you to turn your goat's milk yogurt into that creamy delicacy known as chèvre or **GOAT CHEESE** (page 31). Using goat cheese will open your culinary world to a whole host of new dishes such as **WARM PECAN-CRUSTED GOAT CHEESE ON ORGANIC GREENS** (page 111) and **GOAT CHEESE AND CARAMELIZED ONION TART** (page 105). If you are sensitive to dairy, we suggest you use a dairy-free yogurt starter such as ProGurt or CulturAid (see **RESOURCES** on page 211). If you can tolerate cow's milk, use the same starter you would to make regular **YOGURT** (page 27).

8 cups (2 L) **pasteurized goat's milk**

½ cup (125 mL) **plain store-bought yogurt**, 2 packages (10 mL) **powdered yogurt starter**, or ¼ tsp (1 mL) **dairy-free yogurt starter**

1. Heat the goat's milk in a clean pot over medium heat until the temperature reaches 180°F (82°C). Goat's milk is more delicate than cow's milk and should not be heated above this temperature. When it has reached 180°F (82°C) immediately remove it from the stove.

2. Allow the milk to cool to room temperature or colder, between 64 and 75°F (17 and 24°C). You can refrigerate it to speed up the process.

3. Follow the instructions that relate to the starter you are using.

    a. If you are using **plain yogurt as a starter**:

      Pour 1 cup (250 mL) of the prepared milk or cream into a clean bowl, add ½ cup (125 mL) yogurt, and mix well.

    b. If you are using **powdered yogurt starter**:

      Pour 2 packages (10 mL) of starter into a bowl and add 1 cup (250 mL) of the prepared milk or cream. Mix well.

continued on next page

c. If you are using the **dairy-free yogurt starter**:

Add ¼ tsp (1 mL) of the dairy-free yogurt starter to ¼ cup (60 mL) of the prepared milk and stir until dissolved. Add another ¼ cup (60 mL) of the prepared milk to the mixture and stir well.

4. Add the starter-milk mixture to the rest of the cooled milk and combine well. Pour it into a yogurt maker and follow the manufacturer's instructions, **but not for the suggested fermentation time**.

5. Plug in the yogurt maker and **let the yogurt ferment for 24 to 30 hours**. Most people find that 24 hours is enough.

6. After 24 to 30 hours, refrigerate the yogurt for 6 to 8 hours to allow it to firm and thicken.

7. Treat goat's milk yogurt gently because it can separate if stirred too vigorously.

8. Store in the refrigerator for up to 10 days.

GOAT CHEESE

Makes ½ lb (250 g)

Have you ever wondered why goat cheese or chèvre is so expensive? Well, you're about to find out—it takes 8 cups (2 L) of goat's milk to make just ½ lb (250 g) of cheese! However, as anyone who loves goat cheese will readily admit, the cost is well worth it. The same can be said for this recipe; the process involved in changing goat's milk yogurt into goat cheese may be long—it takes a couple of days—but it's not difficult and the results are worth every minute. If you are lactose-intolerant, making goat cheese from goat's milk yogurt opens the door to many wonderful culinary options. Try our **WARM PECAN-CRUSTED GOAT CHEESE** (page 111) on your salad at dinnertime or with grilled peppers in a crêpe wrap (page 48) for lunch. Or simply enjoy this goat cheese spread on a **SUN-DRIED TOMATO AND BASIL CRACKER** (page 97) and topped with **ORANGE-CRANBERRY MARMALADE** (page 39) as an appetizer to serve to your guests. If you are not following the Specific Carbohydrate Diet, feel free to use store-bought goat cheese in any recipe in this book that calls for goat cheese.

8 cups (2 L) **GOAT'S MILK YOGURT** (page 29)

salt to taste (optional)

1. Soak the bag that comes with your yogurt maker in water until it is thoroughly wet. Wring out the excess water so the bag remains damp but not dripping wet.

2. Carefully pour the yogurt into the bag and hang it at room temperature on a cupboard handle or nail with a bowl underneath to catch the drippings. Alternatively, you can use a large, tightly woven dish towel for the same purpose— just gather and tie the ends together, leaving the yogurt to pool and liquid to drip from the bottom.

3. Allow the yogurt to drip until it stops dripping completely, about 1 to 2 days. Because of the time it takes to drip the yogurt, you may feel more comfortable hanging the yogurt in the refrigerator to drip, especially if you live in a warmer climate.

4. When the yogurt has finished dripping, it will still be quite liquid and the next steps must be followed to yield the results you want.

continued on next page

5. Take a large baking sheet and place 2 dish towels on top. Scrape the contents of the dripping bag onto the top dish towel. Using your hands, shape the cheese into a circle about ½-inch (8-mm) thick.

6. Fold over the top dish towel and cover with another.

7. Place the heaviest object you can find on top of this entire package—we use a 25-lb (12-kg) box of almond flour! The point is to wick the remaining moisture away from the yogurt and a heavy weight is essential for doing this. The heavier the weight, the quicker the process.

8. Check every 15 to 30 minutes to see if the cheese is the consistency you want; change towels and repeat step 5 if necessary. This process should take between 15 minutes and 1 hour. Do not let the cheese get too dry because goat cheese should be moist and creamy—dryer than cream cheese but not as dry as block cheese. You should be able to slice it (see **SLICING GOAT CHEESE** on page 112), but it should stick to the knife when you do so.

9. When the cheese reaches the consistency you want, add salt to taste if desired, place on a square of plastic wrap, and roll it into a log. Refrigerate or freeze.

CLARIFIED BUTTER

Makes ½ lb (250 g)

If you are extremely sensitive to lactose, you may want to use clarified butter instead of regular butter. Clarified butter, sometimes called ghee or drawn butter when it is served with lobster, is completely lactose-free and can be bought at some health food stores or prepared according to these instructions.

1. Heat the butter in a small pot until it melts and light-colored milk solids float to the top.

   ½ lb (250 g) **regular butter**

2. Remove the milk solids by scooping them out with a spoon.

3. Pour the rest of the butter through a sieve into a heat-resistant jar. Store in the refrigerator as you would regular butter.

MAYONNAISE

Makes 1¼ cups (310 mL)

This mayonnaise, better than anything that comes in a jar, is light and fresh tasting. It is also the base for a number of recipes in this book. We use it to create **AIOLI** (page 35), **GINGER AIOLI VINAIGRETTE** (page 89), and **APPLE CIDER VINAIGRETTE** (page 92). If you are not following the Specific Carbohydrate Diet, feel free to use store-bought mayonnaise in any recipe in this book that calls for mayonnaise.

1 large **egg**

1 tsp (5 mL) **white vinegar** or **fresh lemon juice**

1 tsp (5 mL) **Dijon mustard**

1 pinch of **salt**

1 pinch of freshly ground **black pepper**

tiny dribble of **honey** (optional)

1 cup (250 mL) **sunflower oil**

1. Place the egg, vinegar or juice, mustard, salt, freshly ground pepper, and honey if desired, in your food processor or standing blender.

2. With the machine running on high, **slowly** drizzle in the oil (see **MAKING PERFECT MAYO** below).

3. If you prefer a thicker mayonnaise, add more oil.

MAKING PERFECT MAYO

The most common complaint about homemade mayonnaise is that the ingredients separate. This happens when you don't add the oil slowly enough to properly emulsify the mixture. The second-biggest complaint is that oil dribbles all over the appliance as it is added in a slow stream. Here is an easy solution that takes care of both problems. Buy a plastic squeeze bottle similar to the kind used to serve ketchup at a delicatessen. They are commonly available at kitchen supply stores. Pour the oil into the squeeze bottle and turn it upside down with the spout sitting in the feeding hole or tube. With the motor running, apply firm pressure to slowly squeeze the oil out of the bottle. Count to 60 in your head while drizzling. If you still have oil left in the bottle after 60 seconds, you are going slowly enough to achieve proper emulsification so that your mayonnaise won't separate.

AIOLI

Makes 1 cup (250 mL)

Aioli is the name given to a garlic-flavored mayonnaise that originated in the Provence region of France. It is versatile and can be used instead of mayonnaise in wraps (page 75), sandwiches, or as a dipping sauce for **ZUCCHINI FRIES** (page 121), crab cakes, **SPICY PEEL-AND-EAT SHRIMP** (page 143), **SEARED TUNA WITH CARROT FRITTERS** (page 145), and meat. This basic aioli recipe includes additional flavor suggestions (see **AIOLI VARIATIONS** below) that will allow you to be adventurous and creative!

1. Place the garlic in your food processor and mince.

2. Add the egg, vinegar or juice, mustard, salt, freshly ground pepper, and honey if desired. With the food processor running on high, **slowly** drizzle in the oil until none is left and the mixture is thick and emulsified (see **MAKING PERFECT MAYO** on page 34).

2 **garlic cloves**

1 large **egg**

1 tsp (5 mL) **white vinegar** or **fresh lemon juice**

1 tsp (5 mL) **Dijon mustard**

1 pinch of **salt**

1 pinch of freshly ground **black pepper**

tiny dribble of **honey** (optional)

1 cup (250 mL) **sunflower oil**

AIOLI VARIATIONS

Try adding any of the following to the finished aioli. This way you can add, blend, and taste to adjust the seasoning with less guesswork:

- horseradish
- ginger
- hot pepper sauce
- cumin
- thyme
- rosemary

PURE VANILLA EXTRACT

Makes 3 cups (750 mL)

Pure vanilla extract, or liquid gold, as we often refer to it, is so expensive you may consider using the artificial stuff simply because the cost seems so prohibitive. But don't. The artificial stuff not only has additives that you just don't want, but it also doesn't impart the same flavor. This recipe for pure vanilla extract is easy, delicious, and won't break the bank. To make homemade vanilla even more economical, buy vanilla beans online (see **RESOURCES** on page 211), and the next time you are flying home from an international destination, buy vodka duty-free.

12 **vanilla beans**

3 cups (750 mL) **vodka**

1. Carefully slice the vanilla beans lengthwise to expose all the tiny seeds.

2. Drop the sliced vanilla beans into the bottle of vodka, making sure that the vodka covers the full height of the beans.

3. Give the bottle a good shake and store in a cool, dark place for 6 to 8 weeks. The longer it sits, the better it gets.

4. If you think of it, give the bottle a shake a couple of times a week to evenly distribute the seeds and enhance the flavor.

5. After 2 months, pour out about 1 cup (250 mL) of the vanilla extract into another container and set it aside for regular baking use. Meanwhile, top off the big bottle with more vodka, add 3 more beans, and store for another couple of months. This step of pouring off and topping up can be repeated again and again, as long as you add more beans and let the mixture sit for the required time.

HONEY SYRUPS

These syrups dilute the overwhelming sweetness and strength of honey and make a perfect topping for pancakes, waffles, and crêpes. The **SIMPLE SYRUP** recipe is courtesy of the Eastern Connecticut Beekeepers Association.

SIMPLE SYRUP
Makes 1½ cups (375 mL)

1. Heat the water in a pot over medium heat.

2. Add the honey just before boiling.

3. Stir well until combined—do not boil.

4. Remove from the heat. Stir in the vanilla and let cool.

5. Keep refrigerated, but serve warm.

½ cup (125 mL) **water**

1 cup (250 mL) **honey**

1 tsp (5 mL) **PURE VANILLA EXTRACT** (page 36)

LEMON OR ORANGE SYRUP
Makes 1 cup (250 mL)

1. Bring the juice, pulp, and honey to a boil in a small pot over medium-high heat.

2. Lower the heat and simmer for 2 minutes.

3. Remove from the stove and let cool.

4. Keep refrigerated, but serve warm.

juice and pulp of 2 **lemons** or juice and pulp of 2 **oranges**

½ cup (125 mL) warmed **honey**

continued on next page

FRUIT SYRUP
Makes 1 cup (250 mL)

½ cup (125 mL) **honey**

½ cup (125 mL) fresh or frozen
chopped fruit—try bananas,
peaches, slices of pre-cooked
apple, or berries

2 Tbsp (30 mL) unsweetened,
unsalted **peanut butter**
(optional)

1. Bring all the ingredients to a boil in a small pot over medium-high heat.

2. Lower the heat and simmer for 2 minutes while stirring.

3. Remove from the stove and let cool.

4. Keep refrigerated, but serve warm.

ORANGE-CRANBERRY MARMALADE

Makes 2 cups (500 mL)

In the cooking classes we teach, this marmalade is one of our students' favorites. It is easy to make and provides an intense orange taste with a hint of vanilla.

1. Zest the tangerines using a rasp zester.

2. Remove the peel and discard the white pith from around the tangerine.

3. Tear the tangerine into segments and remove the seeds.

4. Slice the vanilla bean lengthwise and scrape out the seeds.

5. Combine the tangerine segments and zest with the vanilla bean, vanilla seeds, honey, orange juice, lemon juice, and cranberries in a medium-sized pot over medium heat.

6. Bring the mixture to a boil, reduce the heat, and simmer for 20 minutes.

7. Break the cranberries against the side of the pot using a spoon to further release their pectin.

8. Cook on low until further thickened, about 10 more minutes.

9. Remove the vanilla bean and let cool. The marmalade will continue to thicken while cooling.

10. Store in the refrigerator or freeze (see **FREEZING LEFTOVER JAM** on page 40).

5 sweet **tangerines**

1 **vanilla bean**

½ cup (125 mL) **honey**

1½ cup (375 mL) pure, unsweet-ened **orange juice**

juice of 2 **lemons**

½ cup (125 mL) fresh or frozen **cranberries**

RASPBERRY JAM

Makes 3 cups (750 mL)

Although this recipe is for raspberry jam, an equal combination of strawberries, blueberries, raspberries, and blackberries also work beautifully to produce a great bumbleberry jam if you follow the proportions listed below. But be sure to remember the cranberries regardless of which berries you use—their high pectin content makes them essential for thickening this jam. Feel free to use frozen berries so you can make this recipe all year round.

2 lbs (1 kg) fresh or frozen **raspberries**

1 cup (250 mL) frozen, whole, unsweetened **cranberries**

1¼ cups (310 mL) **honey**

juice of ½ **lemon**

1. Bring the raspberries, cranberries, and honey to a boil in a medium-sized pot over medium heat.

2. Stir and reduce the temperature to low. Simmer for 20 minutes.

3. At the 20-minute mark, stir and break up the cranberries by mashing them against the side of the pot with the back of a spoon. This helps release all their pectin.

4. Raise the temperature to medium and boil for 10 more minutes, stirring occasionally so the jam does not scorch.

5. After 10 minutes, if the mixture is somewhat thick and no longer runny, turn off the heat. It will thicken as it cools. If it is not thick enough, lower the heat and continue cooking, checking minute by minute until it thickens.

6. Squeeze the lemon over the warm jam in the pot and let it cool to room temperature—it will continue to thicken as it cools.

7. Spoon the cool jam into glass jars and refrigerate. This jam can be frozen (see **FREEZING LEFTOVER JAM** below).

FREEZING LEFTOVER JAM

Because homemade jam doesn't have preservatives, you may want to store only small amounts at a time in the refrigerator. If you are cooking for one, consider using ice cube trays to freeze foods (such as jam and tomato paste) that you use in limited amounts. When frozen, pop out the cubes and store them in a plastic bag in the freezer.

OVEN-ROASTED TOMATO SAUCE

Makes 3 cups (750 mL)

When I went to my Uncle Bernie's house to learn how to make his osso buco, he first had me taste the tomato sauce he was using in the recipe. Bernie told me how he made it and I was so overwhelmed by its simplicity that I went home and made it right away, just to make sure he was telling the truth! This recipe is simple and likely the best tomato sauce I have ever tasted, so I decided to share it with you. I now make it and freeze it in batches so that I always have it on hand. Use it in the **OSSO BUCO** (page 156), over Enoki mushrooms to enjoy "pasta" with tomato sauce, or as a base for meat sauce. Use it whenever a recipe calls for tomato sauce. It's delicious! –JB

1. Preheat the oven to 375°F (190°C).

2. Remove the stems from the tomatoes, making a hole through which you can insert the garlic cloves.

3. Stick a garlic clove deep into the hole of each tomato.

4. Rub olive oil all over the tomatoes.

5. Place the tomatoes in an ovenproof bowl and bake for 3 hours, until the tomatoes are completely soft and browned, and the garlic cloves are soft and cooked through.

6. Remove from the oven. With a slotted spoon, leaving all the liquid behind, transfer the garlic-stuffed tomatoes into your food processor or standing blender.

7. Process the tomatoes for about 10 seconds and taste.

8. Season with salt and freshly ground pepper and process again (see **SPICE IT UP!** below).

9. Use straightaway, refrigerate for up to 5 days, or freeze.

12 vine-ripened **tomatoes**, in season

12 whole **garlic cloves**, peeled

olive oil

salt and freshly ground **black pepper** to taste

SPICE IT UP!

To enhance or modify the flavor of this sauce, at step 8 try adding basil, oregano, thyme, or red pepper flakes, or any combination of herbs and spices.

TOMATO PASTE
Makes 1 cup (250 mL)

Although this tomato paste is not as thick as the canned variety, its taste is more delicate. It is used in the **STUFFED BURGERS** (page 161), **CURRY "RISOTTO"** (page 119), and **SHEPHERD'S PIE** (page 163). If you are not following the Specific Carbohydrate Diet, feel free to use store-bought tomato paste in these recipes.

one 48-oz (1.36-L) can of
tomato juice

1. Pour the tomato juice into a medium-sized pot over medium heat.

2. Bring to a boil, watching that it doesn't boil over.

3. Reduce the heat to low. Continue to simmer uncovered, or with a mesh cover or strainer over the opening of the pot to minimize the splatter. You want the moisture in the juice to evaporate, so don't completely cover the pot with a lid.

4. Stir occasionally, reducing the heat as the sauce gets thicker, and continue to cook for about 1¼ hours until it is reduced to 1 cup (250 mL).

5. Refrigerate for up to 2 weeks or freeze.

SPAGHETTI SQUASH

Serves 4 to 6

Spaghetti squash is a wonderful pasta substitute that is also extremely nutritious. It has high levels of vitamins A and C, and more folate and about as much vitamin B6 as regular pasta. You can pre-cook your squash and store it in the refrigerator for up to 4 days.

1. Cut the squash in half. Do not remove the seeds.

2. Place the pieces cut side down in a 10- x 15-inch (4-L) casserole dish.

3. Pour in enough water to fully cover the bottom of the dish.

4. Bake for 50 to 60 minutes at 375°F (190°C) or until the squash pieces feel slightly soft when you press down on them.

5. Turn the squash pieces cut side up and, using an oven mitt to protect your hands from the hot squash, hold the squash steady as you scoop out the seeds with a spoon.

6. Use a fork to scrape out the flesh of the squash, which will come away in strands—just like spaghetti!

7. Mix with any of the toppings listed or use in **"SPAGHETTI" AND MEATBALLS** (page 162).

1 **spaghetti squash**

any of the following toppings: **salt** and **butter**; **Parmesan cheese**; **OVEN-ROASTED TOMATO SAUCE** (page 41); **basil**, **oregano**, **salt**, and **freshly ground black pepper**; **yogurt**; **honey** and **cinnamon**

QUICK COOK!

You can cook squash quickly in the microwave. Depending on the capacity of your microwave, you may have to cook half a squash at a time. Place the squash cut side down on a microwave-safe plate and add enough water to cover the surface of the plate. Cook on high for 8 to 15 minutes or until the squash feels slightly soft when you press down on it. Remove from the microwave and continue with the squash recipe at step 5.

CHICKEN STOCK

Makes 12 cups (3 L)

Chicken soup, the quintessential traditional remedy for everything that ails you, is also one of the essential flavor building blocks for a number of dishes. Chicken stock rounds out and adds a depth of flavor that water simply cannot. But what is the difference between chicken soup and chicken stock? Chicken soup is flavored with salt and pepper and may contain chicken pieces and vegetables. Chicken stock is clear and typically unseasoned. Make this large batch and freeze it in 1- to 2-cup (250- to 500-mL) portions for easy addition to other recipes.

16 cups (4 L) **water**

3 large **carrots**, cut into large chunks

5 **celery stalks**, cut into large chunks

2 medium-sized **onions**, quartered

1 small bunch fresh **parsley**

2 lb (1 kg) **chicken bones**

salt and freshly ground **black pepper** to taste

1. Fill a large soup pot with cold water.

2. Add the carrots, celery, onions, parsley, and chicken bones.

3. Cover the pot and slowly bring to a boil.

4. Reduce the heat to low, cover, and continue to cook for 2 hours.

5. Remove the solid ingredients from the soup and refrigerate. (Often you can make an entire meal from what is left on the bones of the chicken and all the vegetables pulled from the soup.)

6. Simmer **uncovered** for 1 to 3 hours to reduce and concentrate the flavors.

7. Strain the stock through cheesecloth or a clean dish towel to remove any tiny food particles that might still be present.

8. Cool to room temperature before refrigerating.

9. When cooled in the refrigerator, a thin layer of fat will form on top of the stock. This coagulated fat can be easily lifted off and discarded.

10. Now you can portion the stock into containers and freeze for later use.

CHICKEN SOUP

If you want to serve this stock as a soup, follow steps 1 to 9 of the master recipe. Set aside the chicken bones and vegetables that are removed at step 5 and remove any chicken that was left on the bones. Reheat the stock and season with salt and freshly ground pepper. Return the chicken and vegetables to the soup and heat through before serving.

CANDIED PECANS

Makes 1 lb (500 g)

Delicious by the handful, or on top of ice cream (pages 189 to 194) or any of the salads (pages 89 to 93), these candied pecans are easy to make and hard to resist!

1. Preheat the oven to 300°F (150°C) and line a baking sheet with parchment paper.

2. Beat the egg whites in a large bowl until frothy.

3. Add the pecan halves and stir to coat.

4. Add the rest of the ingredients and combine thoroughly.

5. Pour the pecan mixture onto the prepared baking sheet and bake for about 25 minutes until the pecans are brown and dry, stirring every 5 to 10 minutes to prevent burning.

6. Remove from the oven and turn the temperature down to 175°F (85°C).

7. Return the nuts to the oven and bake for 30 more minutes.

8. Turn the oven off and let the pecans cool and harden in the oven.

9. When cool, store the pecans in a sealed container at room temperature or freeze.

1 lb (500 g) **pecan halves**

2 large **egg whites**

¼ cup (60 mL) warmed **honey**

2 tsp (10 mL) ground **cinnamon**

1 pinch of **cloves**

1 pinch of **nutmeg**

¼ tsp (1 mL) **salt**

HONEY PEANUTS

Makes 1 cup (250 mL)

Known for being high in fat and causing severe allergic reactions, peanuts have been much maligned. If you aren't allergic to them, peanuts are a great source of "good" fat (see **GOOD FAT** on page 15), protein, niacin, and folate. Add these healthy, dressed-up peanuts as a garnish to **THAI MANGO SALAD** (page 113) or simply enjoy them for snacking.

1 cup (250 mL) **raw peanuts**

3 Tbsp (45 mL) **honey**

1 pinch of **salt**

1. Preheat the oven to 350°F (180°C) and line a baking sheet with parchment paper.

2. Combine the peanuts, honey, and salt in a small pot over medium heat.

3. Stir until the peanuts are entirely coated with the honey and form a hot, sticky mass.

4. Spread the peanuts on the prepared baking sheet and bake for 15 minutes.

5. Remove the peanuts from the oven and let them cool and harden.

6. Break nut clusters into smaller pieces and store in an airtight container at room temperature or freeze.

SPICED CASHEWS
Makes 1 lb (500 g)

Cashews not only have a much lower fat content than most other nuts, but they are also quite high in copper. We often don't think about copper as an essential nutrient, but this mineral plays an important role in the metabolism of iron, the development of bone and connective tissue, and the production of the hair and skin pigment called melanin. So enjoy these spiced cashews for a snack or toss them in a salad with romaine lettuce and **GINGER AIOLI VINAIGRETTE** (page 89).

1. Preheat the oven to 350°F (180°C).

2. Toss the cashews with the oil in a bowl.

3. Sprinkle with the cayenne pepper and salt, and toss to coat completely.

4. Spread the nuts out evenly on a baking sheet and bake for 10 minutes.

5. Remove from the oven and let cool completely.

6. Store in an airtight container at room temperature or freeze.

1 lb (500 g) **unsalted cashew nuts**

1 tsp (5 mL) **almond**, **peanut**, or **walnut oil**

½ tsp to 1 tsp (2 to 5 mL) **cayenne pepper**

½ tsp (2 mL) **salt**

BASIC CRÊPES

Makes about 12 to 16 crêpes

These versatile crêpes are perfect with just about any filling—sweet or savory. Once you have prepared the batter, the possibilities are endless. We hope that you will try all of the sweet crêpe recipes (pages 63, 64, and 168) and **SANDWICH WRAPS** (pages 75 to 77), which are perfect for breakfast, brunch, lunch, or dinner. We also encourage you to invent your own combinations.

We suggest that when you are making crêpes you use up all the crêpe batter and freeze any unused crêpes for future use (see **FREEZING AND THAWING CRÊPES** below). Halve or quarter the crêpe filling recipes (pages 63 to 65) to make only as much as you need for the number of crêpes that you will be serving.

In terms of presentation, you can either roll the crêpe into a cigar shape with the filling in the middle or you can top each crêpe with filling. Before topping the crêpes with filling, we suggest you fold each crêpe in half and then in half again to make a rounded triangle. Arrange the triangles on a plate with the pointed ends toward the center and spoon on the filling.

5 large **eggs**

½ cup (125 mL) plus 2 Tbsp (30 mL) finely ground **almond flour** (see **FINELY GROUND ALMOND FLOUR** on page 54)

2 Tbsp (30 mL) **water**

2 tsp (10 mL) **honey**

1 pinch of **salt**

melted **butter** to cook the crêpes

1. Add all the ingredients to a large bowl and whisk them together until they are well mixed.

2. Refrigerate for at least 15 minutes so the mixture thickens a bit.

3. Remove the batter from the refrigerator and stir.

4. Cook the crêpes in an omelet pan or use a crêpe maker (see **CRÊPES MADE EASY** on page 49).

FREEZING AND THAWING CRÊPES

The crêpes need to have *two* pieces of foil or parchment paper between each of them because they stick to the foil or parchment paper while frozen. If you freeze your crêpes with only one piece of foil or parchment paper separating them, you will have to thaw the entire stack at once, even if you wish to use just a few.

CRÊPES MADE EASY

One note about cooking crêpes—no matter how adept you are at flipping pancakes, every-one can use a little help making these delicate treats. One of our favorite small appliances is a crêpe maker, which is widely available online or at kitchen stores and looks like a small inverted omelet pan—you just heat it up and dip it into a shallow dish filled with batter. Seconds later, the crêpe is ready to be lifted carefully from the nonstick surface; *voilà*— perfect every time! Depending on the crêpe maker you use, you may have to coax the sides of the crêpe off the top of the pan with the help of a nonstick spatula. The crêpe will then lift off without tearing. Stack the crêpes on a plate between pieces of parchment paper so they don't stick together.

Here's how to make crêpes the traditional way:

1. Place an 8-inch (20-cm) omelet pan over medium heat.

2. Brush the pan with a bit of butter. Use ½ tsp (2 mL) melted butter for each crêpe.

3. Stir the batter to thoroughly incorporate the almond flour. You may have to do this before making each crêpe.

4. Pour 2 Tbsp (30 mL) of crêpe batter into the pan and swirl it around until the bottom of the pan is evenly covered.

5. Cook for less than 1 minute until the crêpe is set but not brown. The batter cooks and burns faster because of the honey.

6. Loosen the sides of the crêpe with a spatula, turn, and cook for only a few seconds on the other side.

7. Remove the crêpe from the pan and stack it on a plate between pieces of parchment paper.

BREAKFAST

Ah, breakfast: the most important meal of the day. Some people don't eat breakfast, but we do. In fact, we love it! Studies also show that eating a healthy breakfast can play an important role in weight control and can help you concentrate better throughout your morning. This section introduces you to all our morning meal favorites, from muffins and waffles to scrambles and crêpes. For more breakfast ideas, see **DESSERT FOR BREAKFAST AND BREAKING OTHER MEALTIME BARRIERS** (page 207).

LEMON-CRANBERRY MUFFINS

Makes 12 regular or 30 mini muffins

These deliciously sweet yet tart muffins are a favorite. Eat them on the run or warm them up at home and enjoy them with a pat of butter.

2½ cups (625 mL) **almond flour**

½ tsp (2 mL) **baking soda**

½ tsp (2 mL) **salt**

3 large **eggs**

1 tsp (5 mL) **PURE VANILLA EXTRACT** (page 36)

½ cup (125 mL) **honey**, warmed

⅓ cup (75 mL) freshly squeezed **lemon juice**

1 cup (250 mL) fresh or frozen **cranberries**, chopped

1. Preheat the oven to 310°F (155°C) and line a muffin or mini muffin tin with baking cups.

2. Combine the almond flour, baking soda, and salt in a bowl.

3. Mix together the eggs, vanilla, honey, and lemon juice in another bowl.

4. Add the dry ingredients to the wet and stir until combined.

5. Mix in the cranberries.

6. Half-fill each baking cup with batter.

7. Bake until a toothpick inserted in the center of a muffin comes out clean, about 18 to 20 minutes.

MUFFIN-MIX MUFFINS

Makes 12 muffins

These muffins taste like they are made with everything that we love to eat but know isn't good for us—all-purpose flour, refined sugar, and saturated fat. However, their taste belies their ingredients—real fruit, wholesome honey, and cholesterol-lowering almond flour. They are loaded with fiber and "good fat" to keep you going all morning.

1. Preheat the oven to 300°F (150°C) and line a muffin tin with baking cups.

2. Mix the almond flour, baking soda, and salt in a bowl.

3. Add the honey, vanilla, and eggs to the flour mixture and whisk together until thoroughly combined and smooth.

4. Add the fruit and mix well.

5. Spoon the batter into the prepared muffin tin and bake until the muffins start to lightly brown and a knife comes out clean when inserted, about 25 to 30 minutes.

2½ cups (625 mL) finely ground **almond flour** (see **FINELY GROUND ALMOND FLOUR** on page 54)

½ tsp (2 mL) **baking soda**

scant ½ tsp (2 mL) **salt**

¼ cup (60 mL) **honey**

1 Tbsp (15 mL) **PURE VANILLA EXTRACT** (page 36)

3 large **eggs**

1 cup (250 mL) fresh or frozen **berries or chopped fruit**—try berries, apple or peach chunks, or banana slices

FINELY GROUND ALMOND FLOUR

If you bake regularly with almond flour, you know that its texture can vary widely and often influences the baking time and finished texture of a dish. If you want to make your coarser almond flour significantly finer, whiz it around for up to 1 minute in your food processor—don't let the flour process too long or you'll get almond butter. This is particularly easy if you are using a food processor to make pie or tart crusts; simply process the flour for up to a minute before you add the other ingredients.

A simple way to tell if your almond flour is already finely ground is to test how easily it clumps together. The method you use depends on whether your almond flour is frozen, refrigerated, or at room temperature. If your almond flour is refrigerated or at room temperature, squeeze some in your hand—if it sticks together and forms a ball, then the flour is finely ground. If it stays loose when you squeeze it, then the flour is coarsely ground. If your flour is frozen and forms lumps that are hard to break apart, then it is finely ground. If your frozen flour has no lumps or the lumps are extremely easy to break loose, then your flour is coarsely ground.

SWEET MORNING POPOVERS

Makes 12 popovers

Best served hot, these simple pastries are light and buttery. I make them with blueberries—a true "super food." Blueberries are very low in calories, but are high in antioxidants, vitamin C, and fiber. You can also turn your popovers into Danish pastries by drizzling them with the glaze used in the **GLAZED POUND CAKE** (page 180). —JL

1. Preheat the oven to 325°F (160°C) and line a baking sheet with parchment paper.

2. Mix the flour, baking soda, and salt in a medium-sized bowl until well combined.

3. Add the butter, honey, vanilla, and eggs and mix until smooth.

4. Stir in the berries or chopped fruit.

5. Form 2-Tbsp (30-mL) balls of dough and place them on the prepared baking sheet about 1 inch (2.5 cm) apart.

6. Bake until the popovers are golden brown, about 12 to 15 minutes.

2 cups (500 mL) **almond flour**

½ tsp (2 mL) **baking soda**

2 pinches of **salt**

½ cup (125 mL) **butter**, melted

2 Tbsp (30 mL) **honey**

½ tsp (2 mL) **PURE VANILLA EXTRACT** (page 36)

2 large **eggs**

½ cup (125 mL) fresh or frozen **berries**

BASIC BISCUITS
Makes 18 to 20 biscuits

These biscuits are melt-in-your mouth good. They are perfect with eggs, **RASPBERRY JAM** (page 40), and butter for breakfast. You can also enjoy them at lunch as a sandwich bun, or for dinner with **CRISPY SOUTHERN CHICKEN** (page 151) or **"SPAGHETTI" AND MEATBALLS** (page 162). They are also delicious if you eat them plain.

2 cups (500 mL) **almond flour**

scant ¾ tsp (4 mL) **salt**

1 large **egg**

½ cup (125 mL) **butter**, softened or partially melted

1. Preheat the oven to 325°F (160°C) and line a baking sheet with parchment paper.

2. Mix the almond flour and salt in a medium-sized bowl.

3. Add the egg and butter and combine well. Knead the dough with your hands—it will be very stiff.

4. Form 2-Tbsp (30-mL) balls of dough and place them on the prepared baking sheet. Flatten the balls slightly with the palm of your hand to form disks. The disks won't spread, so feel free to place them close together.

5. Bake for 18 to 20 minutes.

6. Eat warm or store in the refrigerator in an airtight container.

CHEDDAR CHEESE BISCUITS

Makes 12 to 14 biscuits

These biscuits are delicious spread with **ORANGE-CRANBERRY MARMALADE** (page 39) to simultaneously fulfill your need for something sweet and savory. They also make great sandwich bread when sliced in half horizontally.

1. Preheat the oven to 310°F (155°C) and line a baking sheet with parchment paper.

2. Combine the flour, baking soda, and salt in a bowl.

3. Add the cheddar cheese and onion and toss.

4. Whisk together the egg, honey, yogurt, and water in another bowl.

5. Add the dry ingredients to the wet and stir until thoroughly combined.

6. Using a ⅓-cup (75-mL) measure, form the batter into rounds and flatten slightly to form 2½-inch (6-cm) discs. Space them evenly on the prepared baking sheet. The biscuits will spread a bit so make sure to leave 1 inch (2.5 cm) between them.

7. Bake until nicely browned, about 20 to 30 minutes.

8. Enjoy warm or cool.

3 cups (750 mL) **almond flour**

1 tsp (5 mL) **baking soda**

½ tsp (2 mL) **salt**

6 oz (175 g) **extra old cheddar cheese**, grated

2 small **onions**, chopped

3 large **eggs**

2 Tbsp (30 mL) **honey**

¼ cup (60 mL) **YOGURT** (page 27)

½ cup (125 mL) **water**

COTTAGE CHEESE WITH FRUIT AND CANDIED PECANS

Serves 1

Adding candied pecans to this simple dish transforms it into a breakfast you will really look forward to. Even if you aren't lactose-intolerant, we suggest that you use dry-curd cottage cheese instead of regular cottage cheese because the fruit and nuts in this dish complement the firmer texture of the dry-curd cottage cheese.

1. Combine the dry-curd cottage cheese, strawberries, and apple in a small bowl.

2. Sprinkle with the chopped pecans and enjoy!

¼ cup (60 mL) **dry-curd cottage cheese**

½ cup (125 mL) **strawberries**, sliced

¼ cup (60 mL) **apple**, chopped

2 Tbsp (30 mL) to ¼ cup (60 mL) **CANDIED PECANS** (page 45), coarsely chopped

WAFFLES AND PANCAKES
Makes about 8 small waffles or about 15 pancakes

This gem of a recipe is from our colleague Deanna Goldberg. The batter is quick to make and produces waffles and pancakes that taste exactly like those you used to eat. The pancakes can be a bit hard to flip, so make them small. Be aware that the batter cooks and burns faster because of the honey. The pancakes and waffles also tend to burn if you try to reheat them in a toaster or uncovered in a toaster oven, but they reheat well in the microwave or wrapped in foil in a toaster oven. Serve topped with any of the **HONEY SYRUPS** (pages 37 to 38), plain yogurt or whipped cream made from whipping cream yogurt (see **WHIPPED CREAM** below), berries, banana slices, or any ice cream (pages 189 to 194).

1. Heat the waffle iron or pancake griddle.

2. Mix the almond flour, salt, and baking soda in a medium-sized bowl.

3. Add the eggs, honey, and vanilla to the flour mixture, and combine thoroughly—it is easiest to mix with a whisk. If you would like the batter to be thicker, refrigerate for about 15 minutes or add more almond flour.

4. Spoon the batter onto the hot waffle iron or pancake griddle and cook according to the manufacturer's instructions.

5. Serve immediately or store in the refrigerator or freezer for future use.

1 cup (250 mL) **almond flour**

¼ tsp (1 mL) **salt**

¼ tsp (1 mL) **baking soda**

4 large **eggs**

2 Tbsp (30 mL) **honey**

1 tsp (5 mL) **PURE VANILLA EXTRACT** (page 36)

WHIPPED CREAM

It's easy to make whipped cream from yogurt made from whipping cream. Just beat the whipping cream yogurt with an electric mixer as you would regular whipping cream and add honey to taste.

CRÊPES WITH BRIE CHEESE AND CARAMELIZED APPLE

Serves 4

After returning from a cycling trip through Quebec, I was inspired to create a few crêpe recipes. This recipe is exquisite when the heat from the caramelized apple melts the brie. —JB

1. Peel and core the apples and cut them into thin slices.

2. In a medium-sized frying pan on medium heat, cook the sliced apples and butter until they brown slightly and soften, about 5 to 7 minutes.

3. Add cinnamon to taste. Stir to coat the apples with the cinnamon and remove from the heat.

4. Cut the brie into ¼-inch (5-mm) slices.

5. Fold each crêpe into a triangle. Place 4 folded crêpes on each serving plate with the points facing in and overlapping.

6. Top each plate of crêpes with the slices of brie.

7. Spoon caramelized apples on top of the brie.

8. Top with warmed syrup or your favorite warmed jam.

4 **baking apples** such as Granny Smith, Braeburn, or Golden Delicious

2 Tbsp (30 mL) **butter**

ground **cinnamon** to taste

½ lb (250 g) **brie cheese**

16 **BASIC CRÊPES** (page 48)

warmed **SIMPLE SYRUP** (page 37) or **RASPBERRY JAM** (page 40) (optional)

CRÊPES WITH SAUTÉED PEARS AND RAISINS

Serves 4

These crêpes are perfect for an indulgent, peaceful breakfast alone or to serve to guests for brunch. The warmed raisins offer a wonderful texture to this light, sweet crêpe dish. Add a sprinkle of candied pecans for a beautiful presentation.

4 **pears**

1 Tbsp (15 mL) **butter**

¼ cup (60 mL) **raisins**

16 **BASIC CRÊPES** (page 48)

ground **cinnamon** to taste

¼ cup (60 mL) coarsely chopped **CANDIED PECANS** (page 45) (optional)

warmed **SIMPLE SYRUP** (page 37) or **RASPBERRY JAM** (page 40) (optional)

1. Peel and core pears and slice each into 8 pieces.

2. Sauté the sliced pears in butter in a medium-sized frying pan on medium heat until they soften, about 3 to 5 minutes. Do not overcook or they will begin to fall apart.

3. Add the raisins and warm through.

4. Fold each crêpe into a triangle. Place 4 folded crêpes on each serving plate with the points facing in and overlapping.

5. Spoon the pear and raisin mixture on top of the crêpes and sprinkle with cinnamon and pecans.

6. Top with the warmed syrup or your favorite warmed jam.

HAM AND SWISS CRÊPES

Serves 4

When I was a kid growing up in Montreal, my family used to frequent a restaurant called La Crêpe Bretonne. It was a wonderful place where just the smell of the crêpes when you walked in the door was enough to make your mouth water. One of their most popular crêpes was ham and Swiss cheese served with warm maple syrup. As much as I loved this meal, the idea of putting maple syrup on ham seemed strange to me—I preferred ham with mustard! Years later, when I was experimenting in the kitchen, this idea came floating back to me, and I figured all those Quebecers couldn't be wrong! I am so happy that I was "brave" enough to try this crêpe with syrup—it *really* is delicious. –JB

1. Preheat the oven to 300°F (150°C).

2. Lay the slices of ham so that they completely cover each crêpe.

3. Evenly sprinkle the grated cheese on top of them.

4. Loosely roll each crêpe to make long, thick cigar shapes.

5. Place the crêpes seam side down in a buttered 9- x 13-inch (3.5-L) casserole dish.

6. Bake until the cheese is melted and the crêpes are warmed through, about 7 to 10 minutes.

7. Serve hot from the oven and drizzle with warmed syrup.

16 **BASIC CRÊPES** (page 48)

1 lb (500 g) **smoked ham** with no sugar or additives, thinly sliced

½ lb (250 g) **Swiss Emmenthal** or **Jarlsberg cheese**, grated

warmed **SIMPLE SYRUP** (page 37) to taste

FRITTATA

Makes one 8-inch (20-cm) square

When I tried this light and flavorful dish at a birthday luncheon, I couldn't stop eating it even though it contained a couple of ingredients I don't usually have: sour cream and bread crumbs. I asked my friend Marla Singer if I could adapt her recipe for this book and she generously agreed. This is a wonderful dish to serve your family for breakfast or your friends for brunch. Serve this frittata warm from the oven or bake it, slice it, and freeze the slices individually. For a quick breakfast, pop a serving in the toaster oven or microwave to reheat and you have an easy, delicious breakfast to eat on the run. –JB

½ lb (250 g) **cheddar cheese**, grated

¼ cup (60 mL) **almond flour**

¼ to ½ cup (60 to 125 mL) **Italian parsley**, chopped

1 Tbsp (15 mL) **olive oil**

2 **onions**, chopped

2 **garlic cloves**, pressed

1 **green pepper**, sliced

1 cup (250 mL) **button mushrooms**, sliced

1 **red pepper**, sliced

5 large **eggs**, beaten

½ cup (125 mL) **YOGURT** (page 27)

1 tsp (5 mL) **salt**

¼ tsp (1 mL) freshly ground **black pepper**

1. Preheat the oven to 350°F (180°C).

2. Combine the cheese, almond flour, and parsley in a large bowl.

3. Heat the oil and sauté the onions and garlic in a large frying pan over medium heat until they are fragrant, about 1 or 2 minutes.

4. Add the peppers and mushrooms, and continue to sauté until all the water that accumulated in the pan evaporates.

5. Mix the eggs, yogurt, salt, and freshly ground pepper in a small bowl.

6. Combine all the ingredients in the larger bowl and mix well.

7. Pour the mixture into an 8-inch (2-L) square casserole dish and bake for 40 to 50 minutes until golden brown and fully set.

8. Remove from the oven and let sit for 5 to 10 minutes before serving.

OMELETS AND SCRAMBLES
Serves 1 to 2

Omelets and scrambles are breakfast basics. Here we suggest a few quick and easy vegetarian egg dishes (see below) that will help you to start your morning with energy, vitamins, and protein. You can get creative from there—feel free to toss anything you want in your eggs (well, we don't recommend the kitchen sink). See the next page for basic omelet and scramble cooking methods.

EGGNOG OMELET OR SCRAMBLE

3 **eggs**, beaten with ½ tsp (2 mL) **PURE VANILLA EXTRACT** (page 36) and 2 shakes of ground **nutmeg**

drizzle of **SIMPLE SYRUP** (page 37) to taste

SUNRISE OMELET OR SCRAMBLE

3 **eggs**, beaten

2 tsp (10 mL) **olive oil** or **butter**

¼ cup (60 mL) halved **yellow cherry tomatoes**

¼ cup (60 mL) grated **yellow zucchini**

¼ cup (60 mL) chopped **orange pepper**

¼ cup (60 mL) shredded **havarti cheese**

salt to taste

PIZZA OMELET OR SCRAMBLE

3 **eggs**, beaten

¼ cup (60 mL) chopped **red bell pepper**

¼ cup (60 mL) chopped **mushrooms**

¼ cup (60 mL) shredded **zucchini**

¼ cup (60 mL) chopped **tomato**

¼ cup (60 mL) grated **Parmesan cheese**

salt and freshly ground **black pepper** to taste

WARM FRUIT OMELET OR SCRAMBLE

3 **eggs**, beaten

1 cup (250 mL) fresh sweet **seasonal berries**—any combination of strawberries, blueberries, and raspberries

drizzle of **ORANGE OR LEMON SYRUP** or **SIMPLE SYRUP** (page 37) to taste

BRUNCH IN THE ANNEX OMELET OR SCRAMBLE

3 **eggs**, beaten

1 cup (250 mL) **spinach leaves**

¼ cup (60 mL) chopped **mushrooms**

½ cup (125 mL) sliced **Camembert cheese**

salt and freshly ground **black pepper** to taste

GOURMET OMELET OR SCRAMBLE

3 **eggs**, beaten

½ cup (125 mL) **GOAT CHEESE** (page 31) or sliced **brie**

¼ cup (60 mL) **sun-dried tomato**, chopped

½ tsp (2 mL) dried **oregano**

salt and freshly ground **black pepper** to taste

continued on next page

BASIC OMELET OR SCRAMBLE METHOD

1. Warm the olive oil or butter in an omelet pan on medium heat.

2. If your omelet filling or egg scramble uses fruit, place it in the pan. If it uses vegetables, place them in the pan and add any herbs that will be used.

3. Sauté the vegetables or fruit while stirring until they have softened—vegetables will take about 3 to 5 minutes and fruit about 1 to 2 minutes.

4. **Omelet:** Pour the egg into the pan and cook, pulling the edges of the omelet toward the center, until the top of the omelet begins to set. If adding cheese, sprinkle it on top of the omelet. Fold the omelet in half and continue to cook on medium to medium-low heat until the center is dry.

   Scramble: Pour the egg into the pan and cook while stirring. Cook until the eggs are the texture you prefer, either completely dry or the more traditional moist scram bled eggs. If adding cheese, sprinkle it over the scramble when the eggs are cooked to your liking.

5. Serve immediately.

FRUIT SMOOTHIES
Makes 2 drinks

In March 2006, we were invited to do some consulting at Ste. Anne's Country Inn and Spa in Cobourg, Ontario. The spa's chef, Christopher Ennew, has generously provided a small taste of the culinary treats at Ste. Anne's by allowing us to include two of his recipes in this book: **PINEAPPLE MARMALADE** (page 129) and this fruit smoothie. For breakfast or a snack, smoothies are so easy, especially when you keep a stock of unsweetened frozen fruit in your freezer.

1. Purée all the ingredients in a standing blender for 1 minute.

2. Pour into a chilled glass and garnish with a slice of strawberry and a mint leaf.

1 cup (250 mL) **ice**

juice of 1 large **orange**

¼ cup (60 mL) **YOGURT** (page 27)

8 whole **strawberries**, hulled

½ ripe **banana**, peeled and coarsely chopped

1 slice golden **pineapple**

strawberry slice and **mint leaf** for garnish

continued on next page

FREEZING FRUIT

Frozen fruit is perfect for making extra-thick smoothies because it eliminates the need to add ice. Unsweetened frozen fruit is available at the grocery store or you can freeze your own fresh fruit when it's in season. Follow these instructions to make sure your frozen fruit doesn't stick together and is easy to blend into a smoothie.

1. Line a baking sheet with parchment paper.

2. Slice larger fruit, but leave smaller ones whole. Lay the fruit in a single layer on the prepared baking sheet.

3. Place the baking sheet in the freezer for 1 hour.

4. When the fruit is frozen, transfer it to plastic bags and return it to the freezer. Frozen fruit stays fresh for at least 6 months.

SMOOTHIE VARIATIONS

Makes 2 drinks

Feel free to experiment with your own smoothie taste combinations. You are simply blending fruit and juice—how can you go wrong? Or follow the basic instructions and ingredient suggestions below as a guide. One of our suggestions is to add peanut butter or yogurt to your smoothie. Your drink will taste great with or without these ingredients, but they are excellent sources of protein and can make your smoothie richer in taste and texture. Peanut butter is also a wonderful way to add protein without adding dairy if you have a milk protein allergy or have run out of yogurt.

2 cups (500 mL) **frozen fruit** (see **FREEZING FRUIT** on page 69)

fruit juice to cover

¼ cup (60 mL) **YOGURT** (optional) or 2 Tbsp (30 mL) unsweetened, unsalted **peanut butter** (optional)

1. Scoop frozen fruit into a standing blender.
2. Pour enough juice over the fruit to cover it.
3. Add yogurt or peanut butter.
4. Purée until smooth and enjoy.

HERE ARE SOME OF OUR FAVORITE FRUIT AND JUICE COMBINATIONS:

- raspberries, strawberries, blueberries, unsweetened orange juice
- strawberries, blueberries, banana, unsweetened orange juice
- strawberries, blueberries, mango, unsweetened orange juice
- banana, mango, unsweetened pineapple juice

SMOOTHIE TO SORBET

To turn your smoothie into a sorbet, pour your freshly made smoothie into an ice cream maker and process according to the manufacturer's operating instructions.

LUNCH

Lunch is easy when you plan ahead. Of course you could always eat leftovers! But who needs leftovers when you have biscuits, rolls, and a stack of **BASIC CRÊPES** (page 48) just waiting to be filled? In this section, we provide you with recipes for bread alternatives, as well as soup and salad choices that help round out your lunch. With these options, you can custom-make a light midday snack or a full, hearty meal. For more lunch ideas, see **DESSERT FOR BREAKFAST AND BREAKING OTHER MEALTIME BARRIERS** (page 207).

TWO-MINUTE TUNA SALAD
Serves 6 to 8

This fast and simple tuna salad is mayo-free, but full of flavor. Use it in a sandwich wrap (pages 75 to 77), **TUNA MELT** (page 78), or on a bed of lettuce. For a more traditional tuna salad, particularly to roll in a crêpe, feel free to add **MAYONNAISE** (page 34) to taste.

1. Break up the tuna in a bowl using a fork.

2. Add the rest of the ingredients and mix well.

two 6-oz (170-mL) **cans of tuna**

1 large **tomato**, diced

1 large **red bell pepper**, diced

1 large **cucumber**, diced

½ cup (125 mL) chopped **fresh dill**

1 squeeze of fresh **lemon juice**

salt and freshly ground **black pepper** to taste

SANDWICH WRAPS

Makes 12 to 16, or as many sandwiches as you have crêpes

There was a certain excitement in the air the day we realized that we had discovered grain-free sandwich wraps—frankly, we can't believe it took so long! But the wait was well worth it. Now the possibilities for sandwiches are endless. The concept is quite simple: use **BASIC CRÊPES** (page 48) to make the wraps and roll your favorite filling inside. The crêpes can be made in advance and then frozen (see **FREEZING AND THAWING CRÊPES** on page 48). If you find that some of your rolling ingredients are a little bulky, such as with a steak sandwich, you can double up on the crêpes, stacking one on top of the other to reinforce the wrap.

METHOD

1. Top the crêpe with the sandwich filling of your choice.

2. Roll into a cigar shape and enjoy!

1 batch of **BASIC CRÊPES** (page 48)

fillings to taste (see **SANDWICH WRAP VARIATIONS**, pages 75 to 77)

SANDWICH WRAP VARIATIONS

Here are some great sandwich wrap filling suggestions. We hope you try them all and come up with a few of your own. If you take your lunch to the office, pack the crêpe and the filling separately and assemble just before eating. Pair any of these wraps with a bowl of soup (pages 82 to 88) for a classic soup and sandwich meal.

TUNA AND JARLSBERG

1. Place 1 crêpe on a piece of aluminum foil or microwave-safe plate and top with a piece of Jarlsberg cheese.

2. Heat in the toaster oven or microwave until the cheese is just beginning to melt. Do not brown the edges of the crêpe or it will become brittle and tear during rolling.

3. Add a serving of prepared tuna and roll.

continued on next page

GRILLED VEGGIES AND GOAT CHEESE

1. Carefully spread softened **GOAT CHEESE** (page 31) on a crêpe.

2. Top with grilled vegetables and roll.

FRESH SALMON SALAD

1. Mash leftover **DRY-RUB SALMON BARBECUED ON A CEDAR PLANK** (page 142) with a fork and mix it with chopped green onions, a pinch of cumin, a dollop of **MAYONNAISE** (page 34), and salt and freshly ground pepper to taste.

2. Place the salmon salad on the crêpe, add a piece of romaine lettuce, and roll.

CHICKEN SALAD SANDWICH

1. Chop leftover chicken into small chunks and mix with a dollop of **MAYONNAISE** (page 34), and salt and freshly ground pepper to taste.

2. Spoon the chicken salad on the crêpe and roll.

SPICY CRAB SALAD

1. Drain the liquid from one 7-oz (180-g) can of crab meat.

2. Break up the meat with a fork and mix in a pinch of cayenne pepper, a small dollop of **MAYONNAISE** (page 34), and salt and freshly ground pepper to taste.

3. Spoon the crab salad on the crêpe and roll.

CLASSIC PEANUT BUTTER AND JAM

1. Carefully spread soft peanut butter onto the crêpe.

2. Add homemade **RASPBERRY JAM** (page 40) or **ORANGE-CRANBERRY MARMALADE** (page 39) and roll.

STEAK SANDWICH

1. Spread Dijon mustard on the crêpe (you might need to stack 2 crêpes for this one if you have a lot of filling), and add lettuce and leftover steak.

2. Roll and enjoy.

BACON, LETTUCE, AND TOMATO

1. Spread **MAYONNAISE** (page 34) on the crêpe.

2. Top with lettuce, tomato slices, and a couple of strips of bacon with no sugar added and roll.

TUNA MELT

Makes 1 pizza

This tuna melt uses a gourmet pizza crust variation as its base. It's a great idea to make a few crusts ahead of time, bake them, and freeze them flat between pieces of parchment paper.

½ cup (125 mL) **almond flour**

¼ tsp (1 mL) **salt**

½ tsp (2 mL) **dried basil**

½ tsp (2 mL) **dried oregano**

¼ tsp (1 mL) **dried thyme**

1 tsp (5 mL) **olive oil**

1 large **egg**

TWO-MINUTE TUNA SALAD
(page 73)

cheddar cheese, sliced or grated

1. Preheat the oven to 325°F (160°C). Line a baking sheet with parchment paper and grease with olive oil.

2. Combine the almond flour, salt, basil, oregano, thyme, olive oil, and egg in a mixing bowl. The dough will be the consistency of cookie batter.

3. Spread the dough thinly on the prepared baking sheet to a 6- to 8-inch (15- to 20-cm) diameter.

4. Bake for 10 minutes until the crust is firm and lightly browned.

5. Remove the crust from the oven, and top with the tuna and cheese.

6. Return to the oven and bake until the cheese is melted.

7. Enjoy warm from the oven.

VEGETABLE QUICHE
Serves 6

In our first cookbook, *Grain-Free Gourmet: Delicious Recipes for Healthy Living*, we showed you how to make quiche with a zucchini crust. This quiche uses a more traditional crust made with almond flour and allows you to get creative with the vegetables you use in the filling. We suggest mushrooms, but you can use anything from asparagus to eggplant to peppers to zucchini.

CRUST

1. Preheat the oven to 300°F (150°C).

2. Mix the flour, salt, and baking soda in a bowl.

3. Add the butter and egg to the flour mixture and mix well. The mixture will be crumbly, but continue to knead the dough until it forms a ball.

4. Press the dough into a 9-inch (23-cm) or 10-inch (25-cm) pie plate (it is enough dough to fit either size). Wet your hands with water to help make pressing and spreading the dough easier.

5. Bake until the crust starts to brown slightly, about 10 to 15 minutes.

6. Remove from the oven and let cool.

3 cups (750 mL) **almond flour**

¾ tsp (4 mL) **salt**

¼ tsp (1 mL) **baking soda**

⅓ cup (75 mL) **butter**, melted

1 large **egg**

continued on next page

5 large **eggs**, lightly beaten

½ cup (125 mL) **YOGURT** (page 27)

½ cup (125 mL) grated **Parmesan cheese**

½ cup (125 mL) finely chopped **sweet onion** (try Vidalia onions when they are in season)

2 cups (500 mL) coarsely chopped **mushrooms** (or vegetables of your choice)

1 **garlic clove**, crushed

½ tsp (2 mL) **salt**

1 pinch of freshly ground **black pepper**

1 pinch of **paprika**

FILLING AND ASSEMBLY

1. Preheat the oven to 450°F (230°C).

2. Mix all the ingredients together until fully combined.

3. Wrap the edge of the crust with tin foil to prevent it from burning while cooking.

4. Pour the egg mixture into the crust.

5. Bake for 10 minutes. Then reduce the heat to 350°F 180°C) and bake until the filling is set, about 20 to 30 more minutes. The filling is set when you insert a knife and it comes out clean.

EGG SALAD
Serves 4 to 6

Here is a mayo-free egg salad based on my grandfather's recipe. If you want a more traditional egg salad, feel free to replace the butter with **MAYONNAISE** (page 34). Eat this salad on a bed of spinach or lettuce, in **SANDWICH WRAPS** (page 75), or on **CHEDDAR CHEESE BISCUITS** (page 57). —JL

1. Mash the hard-boiled eggs with a fork to desired consistency.

2. Add the rest of the ingredients and combine well.

6 large **eggs**, hard-boiled (see **MAKING PERFECT HARD-BOILED EGGS** below)

3 Tbsp (45 mL) **butter**, softened

⅓ cup (75 mL) grated **carrot**

⅓ cup (75 mL) finely chopped raw **mushrooms** (your favorite kind)

⅓ cup (75 mL) finely chopped **green onion**

⅓ cup (75 mL) finely chopped **red bell pepper**

salt, freshly ground **black pepper**, and **paprika** to taste

---

MAKING PERFECT HARD-BOILED EGGS

My family loves eggs and finds easy ways to prepare them. My mother's method for making hard-boiled eggs has literally never failed. Her eggs are always the right consistency and easy to peel. They never explode during boiling or have a dark ring around the yolks. Here is her secret:

1. Poke a hole in the fatter end of the eggs with a sterilized pin and put them in a pot.

2. Cover the eggs with cold water and put the pot on a burner with the heat turned to high.

3. Set a timer for 20 minutes. When the timer "dings," your eggs are done.

4. Pour cold water into the pot until the eggs are cool enough to handle.

CARROT SOUP

Makes 12 cups (3 L)

This soup, savory and not too sweet, is loaded with all the goodness of carrots and just a hint of orange and ginger. Everything in the pot is eventually puréed, so for easy preparation, you can grate the carrots using the grating blade of your food processor before adding them to the pot. Alternatively, they may be chopped by hand.

olive oil

1 large **onion**, chopped

2 large **celery stalks**, chopped

1 Tbsp (15 mL) **dried thyme**

2 **garlic cloves**, pressed

1 Tbsp (15 mL) chopped **ginger**

3 lb (1.5 kg) **carrots**, grated or finely chopped

8 cups (2 L) **water**

1½ cups (375 mL) freshly squeezed or unsweetened **orange juice**

salt and freshly ground **black pepper** to taste

1. Drizzle a bit of olive oil in a large soup pot and add the onion, celery, thyme, garlic, and ginger. Sauté until fragrant and the onions are translucent and soft, about 5 minutes.

2. Add the carrots and continue to cook, stirring regularly for 3 more minutes.

3. Add the water and bring to a boil.

4. Lower the heat to a simmer and cover to cook until the carrots are soft and ready to purée, about 30 minutes. If you are using chopped rather than grated carrots, this may take a little longer.

5. Purée the entire soup with an immersion blender or in small batches in a standing blender, returning the soup to the pot when done.

6. Add the orange juice and stir thoroughly.

7. Let simmer for 5 more minutes and taste.

8. Season with salt and freshly ground pepper to taste.

TOMATO SOUP
Serves 6

My friend Lesley Sandler Griff taught me this trick: collect and freeze the rinds left-over from blocks of Parmesan cheese and use them to flavor soup. The rind imparts its Parmesan aroma and flavor without the addition of actual cheese. Try it here with a quick, easy, and delicious tomato soup, a perfect complement to Parmesan cheese. Grate the vegetables using the grating blade of your food processor to simplify preparation. —JB

1. Add the carrots, celery, and onions to a large soup pot over medium heat.

2. Add the garlic and stir until fragrant and heated through, about 5 minutes.

3. Add the tomato juice, water, Parmesan cheese rind, and tomatoes.

4. Bring to a boil and reduce the heat to low.

5. Cover and simmer for 15 minutes or until all the vegetables are soft.

6. Remove the Parmesan rind (it will be a bit melted and may be sticking to the bottom of the pot, so dig deep).

7. Purée the soup with an immersion blender or in small batches in a standing blender, returning the soup to the pot when done.

8. Return the rind to the pot to continue to flavor the soup.

9. Serve garnished with a sprinkling of Parmesan cheese.

1½ lb (750 g) **carrots**, grated or finely chopped

½ lb (250 g) **celery**, grated or finely chopped

1 large **onion**, grated or finely chopped

2 **garlic cloves**, pressed

3 cups (750 mL) **tomato juice**

2 cups (500 mL) **water**

1 oz (30 g) **Parmesan rind**

1½ lb (750 g) **plum tomatoes**, chopped

ROASTED SQUASH AND APPLE SOUP

Serves 6

Back in 2003 when I started Grain-Free JK Gourmet, my baking business, one of the first stores to carry my products was Daiter's Fresh Market in Toronto. Since then, as my business has grown, Daiter's has become the largest supplier of my biscotti, muffins, and granola in the city and, whenever I launch a new product, it is always available at Daiter's before any other store. Daiter's Fresh Market sells products such as specialty cheeses, baked goods, and prepared foods, and they offer a vast selection of original soups that are always delicious. Stephen and Joel Daiter, the brothers who own the store, have been wonderful champions of Grain-Free JK Gourmet, so when I asked them for a recipe for this book, they were only too happy to oblige. This is my favorite Daiter's soup. —JB

½ medium-sized **butternut squash**

1 small **cooking onion**, chopped

1 small **carrot**, chopped

2 **leeks**, chopped

2 **celery stalks**, chopped

3 medium-sized **red apples**, cored, peeled, and chopped

1 handful of **Italian parsley**, chopped

salt and freshly ground **black pepper** to taste

freshly grated **Parmesan cheese** for garnish (optional)

1. Preheat the oven to 375°F (190°C).

2. Place the squash cut side down in a casserole dish and bake until soft, about 40 to 50 minutes.

3. Cover the onion, carrot, leek, and celery with water in a medium-sized pot and cook over high heat.

4. Let the vegetables boil until they are tender.

5. Remove the squash from the oven and, when it is cool enough to handle, remove the flesh from the skin.

6. Add the squash and apples to the pot of soft vegetables and purée with an immersion blender or in small batches in a standing blender, returning the soup to the pot when done.

7. Add the parsley and more water to achieve the thickness you desire and bring back to a boil.

8. Taste and season with salt and freshly ground pepper as necessary and serve sprinkled with Parmesan cheese if desired.

GREEN VEGETABLE SOUP WITH CHICKEN

Serves 6

This soup, appropriately named, uses only green vegetables. The addition of ground chicken makes it a hearty meal all on its own. Prepare this soup ahead of time, and refrigerate it and the cooked ground chicken separately until ready to reheat and serve.

1. Put the vegetables in a large soup pot and add the water.

2. Cover the pot and boil on high for 20 minutes.

3. Lower the heat and purée with an immersion blender or in small batches in a standing blender, returning the soup to the pot when done.

4. Add the chicken stock and increase the temperature. Let simmer for 5 minutes.

5. Brown the ground chicken in a large frying pan with the garlic, salt, and freshly ground pepper.

6. Drain the cooked chicken of its fat.

7. To serve, heat 2 cups (500 mL) of soup and ¾ cup (175 mL) ground chicken per person in a medium-sized pot. Double or triple the proportions as necessary.

1 lb (500 g) **broccoli**, coarsely chopped

1 lb (500 g) **asparagus**, woody ends snapped off and coarsely chopped

4 cups (1 L) coarsely chopped **celery**

1 lb (500 g) **zucchini**, peeled and coarsely chopped

½ lb (250 g) **green bell pepper**, coarsely chopped

2 cups (500 mL) **Italian parsley**, coarsely chopped

5 cups (1.25 L) **water**

4 cups (1 L) **CHICKEN STOCK** (page 44)

2 lb (1 kg) ground **chicken**

2 **garlic cloves**, pressed

salt and freshly ground **black pepper** to taste

RED LENTIL SOUP
Serves 6

This soup doesn't take long because, unlike other legumes, red lentils soften fairly quickly and, other than soaking, don't need any preparation before adding them to the soup. Red lentils cook down nice and soft, leading to a wonderfully thick soup that is hearty enough for a meal—lunch or dinner. As with all soups, avoid the risk of over-seasoning by waiting until the end to add extra salt and freshly ground pepper.

2 cups (500 mL) **red lentils**, soaked and rinsed (see **BEANS AND LEGUMES** on page 87, steps 1 to 3)

1 Tbsp (15 mL) **olive oil**

4 **garlic cloves**, minced

1 large **onion**, finely chopped

2 **carrots**, finely chopped

2 **celery stalks**, finely chopped

8 cups (2 L) **water**

1 tsp (5 mL) **salt** to start and then more to taste

freshly ground **black pepper** to taste

hot pepper sauce for garnish (optional)

1 chopped **tomato** for garnish (optional)

1. Heat the olive oil and add the garlic, onions, carrot, and celery in a large soup pot on medium heat. Sauté for 5 minutes until aromatic.

2. Add the lentils and the water. Bring to a boil and then reduce the heat.

3. Cook covered over low heat for 45 minutes.

4. Lower the heat and purée half the mixture, using either an immersion blender or in small batches in a standing blender, returning the soup to the pot when done.

5. Taste and season with salt and freshly ground pepper.

6. Serve garnished with a couple of dashes of hot pepper sauce and a sprinkle of chopped tomato.

BEANS AND LEGUMES—EASIER TO DIGEST

Beans, split peas, lentils, and peanuts all belong to the legume family. To minimize the bloating, gas, or discomfort you sometimes get with eating prepared legumes, try soaking them.

1. Put dried legumes in a large bowl and cover with water. Make sure the water level is 4 inches (10 cm) above the legumes because they will absorb the liquid, expand, and double in bulk.

2. Soak in a cool place for 8 to 10 hours or overnight in the refrigerator.

3. Drain and rinse in a colander with cool, fresh water.

4. Put the legumes in a large pot, cover with water, and bring to a boil.

5. As soon as the legumes come to a boil, the water will start to foam. Remove from the heat, drain, and rinse the legumes again. This step can be omitted when preparing lentils, which cook too quickly to require a second rise. **At this point, they can be added to soups for further cooking. To fully cook the beans and store for future use, follow steps 6 and 7**.

6. Put the legumes back in your pot and cover them with fresh water again. Boil for 30 to 45 minutes, or until they are tender.

7. Drain and use immediately, or freeze in smaller portions for use in other recipes.

SPLIT PEA SOUP WITH FLANKEN

Serves 6

Flanken, the Yiddish word for short ribs or braising ribs, fills this soup with wonderful flavor. When my grandmother first taught me this recipe, I learned what most people find out when cooking with their grandmothers … there are no measurements! It has always been a source of pride that I was the keeper of my grandma's famous soup recipe, and now I happily share it with you. The original recipe called for barley along with the split peas but, over the years, I dropped the barley and, as you will see, it now has all the measurements you will need to make it a favorite with your family. —JB

3 cups (750 mL) **green split peas**, soaked and rinsed (see **BEANS AND LEGUMES** on page 87, steps 1 to 5)

16 cups (4 L) **water**

1 lb (500 g) **beef short ribs**, on the bone

1 lb (500 g) **carrots**, chopped

1 lb (500 g) **celery**, chopped

1 lb (500 g) **cooking onions**, quartered

fresh dill, coarsely chopped

2 tsp (10 mL) **red wine vinegar**

1 **garlic clove**, minced

salt and freshly ground **black pepper** to taste

1. Heat the water in a large soup pot over medium heat. Add the short ribs and the split peas and bring to a boil. As the water boils, fat and foam from the beef will rise to the top. As this happens, spoon it off and discard.

2. Purée the raw carrots, onions, and celery with a bit of water from the pot in small batches in a standing blender. The carrots will be the most difficult to blend and may need up to 2 cups (500 mL) of water to achieve a purée. Add the blended mixture back to the pot.

3. Let the soup boil uncovered for 1 to 2 hours until the peas are completely soft.

4. Add the dill, vinegar, and garlic.

5. Continue to simmer uncovered until the soup reaches the thickness you want and the meat is falling from the bone.

6. Add salt and freshly ground pepper to taste and serve.

FRESH DRIED LEGUMES

Surprisingly, split peas and beans do have a shelf-life and can get old just sitting around your pantry. Unfortunately, you will only know your split peas are old after you are half-way through making a soup and you find that no matter how long they boil, they just won't soften—trust me, it's happened … more than once! For this reason, buy a new bag of peas when you need them and throw out split peas that are older than 4 months. —JB

CAESAR SALAD WITH GINGER AIOLI VINAIGRETTE

Serves 4

This salad dressing is light and creamy with more than a hint of garlic and ginger. In this recipe, the spiced cashew nuts lend a sweetness that complements the spiciness of their seasoning and the garlic in the dressing.

GINGER AIOLI VINAIGRETTE

Makes ¾ cup (175 mL)

1. Combine the mayonnaise and the vinegar in a small bowl.

2. Add the garlic and ginger and mix thoroughly.

3. Taste the dressing and add salt and freshly ground pepper if necessary.

4. Let sit in the refrigerator for at least 1 hour before using to let the flavors fully develop.

½ cup (125 mL) **MAYONNAISE** (page 34)

3 Tbsp (45 mL) **white vinegar**

1 **garlic clove**, pressed

2 tsp (10 mL) **ginger**, freshly grated

salt and freshly ground **black pepper** to taste

SALAD AND ASSEMBLY

1. Sprinkle the lettuce with the Parmesan cheese and add the dressing to taste.

2. Toss well.

3. Top with the nuts and serve.

4. Refrigerate the leftover dressing.

2 to 3 **romaine lettuce hearts**, washed and chopped

¼ to ½ cup (60 to 125 mL) grated **Parmesan cheese**

½ cup to 1 cup (125 to 250 mL) **SPICED CASHEWS** (page 47)

AN EASY WAY TO PEEL GINGER

The skin on ginger is easy to peel if you scrape it off with the tip of a spoon. Simply run the tip of the spoon down the side of the piece of ginger and the peel comes off with no fuss and no waste.

ROMAINE LETTUCE WITH "ENGLISH" FRENCH SALAD DRESSING

Serves 4

This recipe is so named because it is what *French* salad dressing is called in Britain. Enjoy this garlicky salad with a wrap or soup.

"ENGLISH" FRENCH SALAD DRESSING
Makes about 1¼ cups (310 mL)

1 cup (250 mL) **sunflower oil**

½ cup (125 mL) **apple cider vinegar**

½ tsp (2 mL) **honey**

½ tsp (2 mL) **salt**

¼ tsp (1 mL) **dried basil**

1 **garlic clove**, sliced

1 tsp (5 mL) **paprika**

½ tsp (2 mL) **Dijon mustard**

1 Tbsp (15 mL) grated **onion**

1. Put all the ingredients in a jar with a tight-fitting lid.

2. Shake and let sit for 15 minutes to allow the flavors to intensify.

SALAD AND ASSEMBLY

2 to 3 **romaine lettuce hearts**, washed and chopped

½ cup (125 mL) grated **Parmesan cheese**

¼ cup (60 mL) **sunflower seeds**

1. Sprinkle the lettuce with Parmesan cheese and sunflower seeds.

2. Remove the garlic, add dressing to taste, and toss.

3. Refrigerate the leftover dressing.

MANDARIN SALAD WITH CITRUS VINAIGRETTE

Serves 2

The lovely, light-tasting salad dressing in this recipe works well on lighter lettuces, such as organic greens, baby spinach, and Boston lettuce.

CITRUS VINAIGRETTE

Makes ¾ cup (175 mL)

1. Combine all the ingredients in a jar with a tight-fitting lid.

2. Shake well.

juice of 1 **lime**

juice of 1 **lemon**

1 Tbsp (15 mL) finely chopped **shallot**

1 Tbsp (15 mL) **Dijon mustard**

1 Tbsp (15 mL) **honey**

¼ cup (60 mL) **olive oil**

SALAD AND ASSEMBLY

1. Add the orange segments, raisins, and sunflower seeds to the lettuce.

3. Pour dressing onto the greens to taste and toss well.

4. Refrigerate leftover dressing.

organic greens, **Boston lettuce**, or **baby spinach**, washed and dried well

2 **mandarin oranges**, peeled and divided into segments

¼ cup (60 mL) **raisins**

¼ cup (60 mL) **sunflower seeds**

SALAD WITH TOASTED PINE NUTS, GOAT CHEESE, AND APPLE CIDER VINAIGRETTE

Serves 4

Pine nuts are the seeds that come from the cones of a certain variety of pine tree. The nuts are delicate in taste and texture and are usually quite expensive because of the labor-intensive way in which they are harvested. Luckily, a few nuts go a long way. Try this light and creamy salad dressing on any salad made with romaine lettuce. Feel free to use store-bought goat cheese if you don't follow the Specific Carbohydrate Diet.

APPLE CIDER VINAIGRETTE

Makes ¾ cup (175 mL)

½ cup (125 mL) **MAYONNAISE** (page 34)

3 Tbsp (45 mL) **apple cider vinegar**

2 Tbsp (30 mL) **seedy Dijon mustard** with no sugar added

salt and freshly ground **black pepper** to taste

1. Combine the mayonnaise and the apple cider vinegar.

2. Add the mustard and combine thoroughly.

3. Taste and add salt and freshly ground pepper if necessary.

SALAD AND ASSEMBLY

2 hearts of **romaine lettuce**, washed, chopped, and dried well

¼ cup (60 mL) **cherry** or **grape tomatoes**, halved

¼ cup (60 mL) toasted **pine nuts** (see **TOASTING PINE NUTS** on this page)

¼ cup (60 mL) **raisins**

2 oz (60 g) **GOAT CHEESE** (page 31)

1. Add the tomatoes, pine nuts, raisins, and goat cheese to the lettuce and toss with the dressing to taste.

2. Refrigerate the leftover dressing.

> **TOASTING PINE NUTS**
>
> Pine nuts are easy to toast in your oven or toaster oven. Lay them in a single layer on a baking sheet lined with aluminum foil or parchment paper. Heat at 250 to 300°F (120 to 150°C) until lightly browned. Sprinkle them warm or cold over salad.

AVOCADO WALDORF SALAD

Serves 6 to 8

The dense avocado, sweet and juicy apple, and crisp celery are a great combination in this variation of a Waldorf salad.

1. Toss all of the ingredients in a large bowl.

2. Drizzle with the citrus vinaigrette and serve.

2 **apples**, coarsely chopped

1 **avocado**, diced

5 to 6 **lettuce leaves**, torn into
   bite-sized pieces

2 **celery stalks**, coarsely chopped

¾ cup (175 mL) **chopped pecans**

CITRUS VINAIGRETTE (page 91)

DINNER

You may eat breakfast on the go and then eat lunch at your desk, but dinner is the one meal you are most likely to make time to sit down and enjoy with family or friends. Dinner is more than just a meal—it gives you a chance to unwind at the end of a long day and reconnect with loved ones. In this section, you will find all the dishes you need to round out dinnertime: starters, sides, and main courses. So whether you are eating alone, serving supper to your family, or having company over for an elegant dinner, you should find all the inspiration you need for both simple everyday meals and elaborate entertaining. For more dinner ideas, see **DESSERT FOR BREAKFAST AND BREAKING OTHER MEALTIME BARRIERS** (page 207).

STARTERS

SUN-DRIED TOMATO AND BASIL CRACKERS

Makes about 10 dozen crackers

If you enjoyed the Sesame Dijon Crackers in our first cookbook, *Grain-Free Gourmet: Delicious Recipes for Healthy Living*, you know how easy it is to make fabulous homemade crackers. And if you haven't tried making your own crackers ... what are you waiting for? Here is another recipe that uses the same technique, but produces crackers with a completely different flavor. As before, the instructions are detailed and following them carefully will ensure success. Be sure to return the crackers to the oven for a second baking—it will make your crackers crisp! You will need 2 paper towel tubes to shape this dough.

CRACKERS

1. Place the sun-dried tomatoes in a bowl and cover them with boiling water to reconstitute them; it will take about 20 minutes. When they are soft, drain them and discard the water. Chop the tomatoes very fine.

2. Combine the almond flour, Parmesan cheese, basil, salt, and baking soda in a large mixing bowl.

3. Blend the eggs with the dry-curd cottage cheese or yogurt cheese using your food processor or standing blender, or by hand until the mixture is smooth.

4. Add the dry ingredients to the wet and mix well by hand.

5. Add the sun-dried tomatoes and incorporate them fully into the cheese mixture, using your hands if necessary.

6. Divide the dough in half and shape each half into a log. Wrap each log in plastic wrap and roll it back and forth until the log is long and narrow enough to slide into a paper towel tube.

7. Place each log in a paper towel tube. With the dough inside, place your palms on either end of the tube. Shake it from side to side so the cracker dough expands to fill the space. Put the tubes in the freezer until the dough is frozen.

1 oz (30 g) **sun-dried tomatoes**, before being reconstituted

boiling **water** to cover

2½ cups (625 mL) **almond flour**

1¼ cups (310 mL) grated **Parmesan cheese**

2 tsp (10 mL) **dried basil**

½ tsp (2 mL) **salt**

½ tsp (2 mL) **baking soda**

2 large **eggs**

¾ cup (175 mL) **dry-curd cottage cheese** or **YOGURT CHEESE** (page 28)

salt for sprinkling

continued on next page

BAKING

1. Preheat the oven to 325°F (160°C) and line a baking sheet with parchment paper.

2. Remove 1 tube from the freezer and allow it to sit at room temperature until it is just soft enough to slice, but not too soft, about 10 minutes.

3. To slice, keep the dough in the tube, moving it out of the tube 2 inches (5 cm) at a time while you slice—this will keep the warmth of your hands from softening the batter. With a thin, sharp knife (a boning or filleting knife works well) cut into ⅓-inch (8-mm) slices and place on the prepared baking sheet. You can place them close together—they will barely spread.

4. Bake for 8 minutes.

5. Remove the pan from the oven and turn the crackers over. Bake for 6 more minutes.

6. Remove from the oven and allow the crackers to cool on the baking sheet. Reduce the oven temperature to 175°F (85°C).

7. When the crackers are cool, return them to the oven for 30 to 60 minutes, until they are entirely crisp. Turn off the heat and let the crackers cool in the oven. Multiple batches can be piled up for crisping on 1 baking sheet. This double baking method ensures crackers will be crisp and stay crisp while stored in an airtight container or bag.

8. Serve these crackers as you would any other. We love them spread with **GOAT CHEESE** (page 31), topped with **ORANGE-CRANBERRY MARMALADE** (page 39), or piled high with **CHOPPED LIVER** (page 103).

LACE CRACKERS

Makes 48 crackers

Named for the pattern they create when baked, these crackers are tasty but very delicate. Use them to garnish a salad or simply as a "betcha can't eat just one" kind of snack. You will need 1 paper towel tube to shape this dough.

1. Using your hands, mix all the ingredients well and form into a ball.

2. Place the dough on a piece of plastic wrap and shape it into a log that is long and narrow enough to slide into a paper towel tube. Wrap the log in plastic wrap.

3. Slide the log into a paper towel tube. With the dough inside, place your palms on either end of the tube. Shake it from side to side so the cracker dough expands to fill the space. Put the tube in the freezer until the dough is frozen.

4. Preheat the oven to 350°F (180°C) and line a baking sheet with parchment paper.

5. Allow the crackers to soften for 7 to 10 minutes, long enough to be able to cut through them easily. Slice the crackers ⅓ inch (8 mm) thick and place them 1 inch (2.5 cm) apart on the prepared baking sheet.

6. Bake until lightly browned, about 8 to 10 minutes.

7. Remove from the oven and let cool.

8. Store in an airtight container.

3 oz (90 g) **butter**, at room temperature

½ lb (250 g) **medium cheddar cheese**, grated

1½ cups (375 mL) **almond flour**

⅓ cup (75 mL) **sesame seeds**

½ tsp (2 mL) **hot pepper sauce**

½ tsp (2 mL) **salt**

BAKED BRIE

Serves 6 to 8

This hors d'oeuvre is easy and always a hit with company. Serve it with sliced apples and pears, or **SUN-DRIED TOMATO AND BASIL CRACKERS** (page 97).

1. Preheat the oven to 375°F (190°C).

2. Combine the apple, almonds, raisins or apricots, and your choice of marmalade, jam, or honey in a medium-sized bowl.

3. Slice the brie round in half horizontally and place the bottom half, rind side down, in a round casserole dish.

4. Spoon half the apple mixture over the brie in the casserole dish.

5. Cover with the second half of the brie.

6. Top with the rest of the apple mixture.

7. Bake until the cheese softens around the edges, about 12 to 15 minutes.

8. Remove from the oven and serve warm.

1 **Granny Smith apple**, peeled and chopped into small chunks

⅓ cup (75 mL) **whole roasted almonds**, chopped

⅓ cup (75 mL) **raisins** or chopped **apricots** (about 10)

¼ cup (60 mL) **ORANGE-CRANBERRY MARMALADE** (page 39) or **RASPBERRY JAM** (page 40) or **honey**

one 16-oz (450-g) **round brie cheese**

assorted **crackers** and **sliced apples** and **pears** for serving

CHEESE FONDUE

Serves 4 as an appetizer

Cheese fondue was one of my favorite quintessential après-ski dishes when I was a little girl. Long-abandoned when I gave up eating bread, I added it back into my diet when I realized that it was a wonderfully easy appetizer to serve to company using sliced fruit and vegetables instead of bread for dipping. So resurrect the old fondue pot that you hid away back in the 1970s, and try to find a kirschwasser (cherry brandy) that is fermented without the addition of sugar. Although only 1 tsp (5 mL) is called for in this recipe, the kirschwasser, which, like many liqueurs, can be stored for years in your cupboard, makes this dish taste like the real Swiss deal. —JB

FONDUE

1 **garlic clove**, sliced in half

½ cup (125 mL) **dry white wine**

7 oz (200 g) **Swiss Emmenthal cheese**, coarsely grated

7 oz (200 g) **Gruyère cheese**, coarsely grated

1 tsp (5 mL) **kirschwasser**

FOODS FOR DIPPING

apples, sliced

pears, sliced

cauliflower florets

broccoli florets

mushrooms

1. Rub the bottom and sides of a heavy-bottomed pot with the garlic. Discard the garlic.

2. Add the white wine to the pot and bring to a simmer over medium heat.

3. Slowly add the grated cheese, a handful at a time, and cook over a steady heat without boiling. While adding the cheese, stir in a zigzag motion rather than in a circular motion to prevent the cheese from forming a ball.

4. Continue to add the cheese and stir until all the cheese is melted and creamy.

5. Stir in the kirschwasser.

6. Transfer to a fondue pot over an open flame and serve.

CHOPPED LIVER
Makes about 1 lb (500 g)

If you have never tried liver, or you turn up your nose at the idea of eating liver, you have to try this recipe before you pass judgment. I first tried chopped liver as a kid and hated it; it was heavy and thick and way too liver-y! Then one of my sisters swore that her mother-in-law made the best chopped liver—light and flavorful and without the addition of a single bread crumb—perfect for my grain-free diet. When I called Luiba Grossman, my sister Jennifer's mother-in-law, she generously dictated her recipe to me right there on the phone. The next day, I couldn't wait to get into the kitchen and try it out. To accommodate my own palate, I changed it a bit—slightly more onion and egg to a little less liver—and I adore the results. —JB

1. Wash the chicken livers and boil them in water until cooked through, about 30 minutes. Drain.

2. While the livers are cooking, fry the onions in a bit of oil until they are golden brown.

3. Blend the liver, onions, and hard-boiled eggs in your food processor. Do not over-blend or the chopped liver will be pasty. Just pulse a few seconds at a time, stirring with a spatula every now and then to make sure the ingredients are mixing evenly.

4. If the chopped liver is a little dry, add a bit of warm water to loosen it up.

5. The taste of the chopped liver changes with its temperature and you run the risk of overseasoning if you add salt and pepper when it's warm. For this reason, refrigerate until completely cool and then season if necessary. Be careful not to over-salt. You want the flavor of the sweet onions to come through.

6. Serve with **SUN-DRIED TOMATO AND BASIL CRACKERS** (page 97). This chopped liver will keep in the refrigerator for 3 to 4 days or it can be frozen and thawed overnight in the refrigerator without losing any of its flavor or texture.

1 lb (500 g) **chicken livers**

oil for frying

2 large **sweet onions** (try Vidalia onions when they are in season), diced

3 large **eggs**, hard-boiled (see **MAKING PERFECT HARD-BOILED EGGS** on page 81)

salt and freshly ground **black pepper** to taste

GOAT CHEESE AND CARAMELIZED ONION TART

Makes 6 tarts

These free-form tarts are the perfect appetizer for a dinner party. You can make the tarts ahead of time, refrigerate them, and pop them in the oven just before serving. Garnished with sliced figs and a drizzle of honey, this appetizer is a real crowd-pleaser.

CRUST

1. Process all the crust ingredients in your food processor until thoroughly combined.

2. Divide the dough into 6 equal portions and roll them between 2 small pieces of parchment paper into flat rounds measuring 5 to 6 inches (12 to 15 cm) in diameter.

3. Place the rounds, still on the parchment paper, on a baking sheet and chill them in the refrigerator while you prepare the filling.

1½ cups (375 mL) finely ground **almond flour** (see **FINELY GROUND ALMOND FLOUR** on page 54)

3 Tbsp (45 mL) cold **unsalted butter**

1 tsp (5 mL) **honey**

¼ tsp (1 mL) **salt**

½ tsp (2 mL) **baking soda**

FILLING

1. Cut the onions in half and remove the skin. Slice the onions vertically as thin as possible into half moons.

2. Heat the oil in a frying pan on medium heat and add the onions. Pan fry, stirring frequently for about 20 minutes, until they are soft and browned. If the pan dries out, add 1 Tbsp (15 mL) of water to prevent burning.

3. Remove the onions from the heat and let them cool.

2 large **sweet onions**

olive oil

6 oz (175 g) **GOAT CHEESE** (page 31)

continued on next page

ASSEMBLY AND BAKING

4 to 6 **figs**, sliced

1 Tbsp (15 mL) **honey**, warmed

1. Preheat the oven to 325°F (160°C).

2. When the onions are cool enough to handle, remove the tart crusts from the refrigerator.

3. Lift one of the chilled crusts, still on the parchment paper, and place it on the countertop in front of you.

4. Scoop ⅓ cup (75 mL) of the onion and place it in the center of the pastry round.

5. Crumble 1 oz (30 g) of the goat cheese on top of the onions.

6. Use the parchment paper to help fold the dough up and around the filling, turning the parchment paper as you go. Pinch together any tears in the dough. Return the mini tart, still on the parchment paper, to the baking sheet and repeat the process with the remaining rounds.

7. Top each round with slices of fig and drizzle with ½ tsp (2 mL) of warmed honey.

8. Bake the tarts until the crust is lightly brown, about 20 to 25 minutes.

9. Serve warm.

SPINACH AND CHEESE TRIANGLES

Makes 50 pieces

A great hors d'oeuvre for company, this dish is delicious and easy to make. It can also be made days ahead of time and frozen—simply bake for half the time, cool, and freeze. When ready to finish baking, remove the casserole dish from the freezer but do not thaw. Pop it into the oven and bake for 30 more minutes. If you fully baked this starter before freezing, simply thaw, cut, and warm the triangles through in an oven heated to 250°F (120°C).

1. Preheat the oven to 325°F (160°C).

2. Using your hands, squeeze the excess liquid from the spinach.

3. Combine the spinach and cheeses in a bowl.

4. In another bowl, combine the almond flour, salt, and baking soda.

5. Add the almond flour mixture to the spinach-cheese mixture. Toss to combine thoroughly.

6. Add the beaten eggs and mix well.

7. Pour the entire mixture into a buttered 8-inch (2-L) square casserole dish and bake until cooked through, about 45 minutes.

8. Remove from the oven and let cool slightly.

9. Slice into 25 squares and then slice each square diagonally into triangles. Serve warm.

two 10-oz (300-g) packages of chopped **frozen spinach**, thawed

¼ lb (125 g) medium **cheddar cheese**, grated

¼ lb (125 g) **Parmesan cheese**, grated

½ cup (125 mL) **almond flour**

1 tsp (5 mL) **salt**

1 tsp (5 mL) **baking soda**

4 large **eggs**, lightly beaten

GOURMET PIZZA WITH POACHED PEAR, CARAMELIZED ONION, AND GORGONZOLA CHEESE

Makes 1 pizza

When our first cookbook, *Grain-Free Gourmet: Delicious Recipes for Healthy Living*, was published, Jenny and I went to Vancouver for a short publicity tour—a couple of TV appearances, a magazine interview, and a cooking class. There we met Adrienne O'Callaghan, a food stylist who was assisting us for the day. Adrienne had prepared in advance all the dishes that we were going to be demonstrating so they never actually had to be baked on live TV ... ah, the magic of television. During our first TV appearance, Adrienne improvised an outstanding dish using our pizza crust recipe and I couldn't wait to get home to replicate it. I adore this pizza, which is perfect for lunch, dinner, or, my favorite, as an hors d'oeuvre for company. Everyone loves this dish and your friends will be no exception. To double the recipe, simply double all of the ingredients; to triple the recipe, triple all of the ingredients except for the eggs—use 2 instead of 3; to quadruple the recipe, quadruple everything except for the eggs—use 3 instead of 4. —JB

POACHED PEARS

½ cup (125 mL) **dry white wine**

2 Tbsp (30 mL) **honey**

ground **cinnamon** to taste

ground **cloves** to taste

1 **pear**, peeled and sliced into 8 pieces

1. Combine the white wine, honey, cinnamon, and cloves in a small pot.

2. Add the pear and bring to a simmer.

3. Simmer until tender, about 15 minutes, depending on the firmness of the pear.

4. Strain the pear from the liquid and set aside.

CARAMELIZED ONIONS

1 large **cooking onion**, sliced

1½ tsp (7 mL) **butter**

sunflower oil

1. Add the onion, butter, and a bit of oil to a frying pan over medium heat.

2. Cook the onion, stirring frequently for about 20 minutes, until it is soft and browned. If the pan dries out, add 1 Tbsp (15 mL) of water to prevent burning.

3. Remove the onion from the heat and let it cool.

PIZZA CRUST AND ASSEMBLY

1. Preheat the oven to 325°F (160°C) and line a baking sheet with parchment paper.

2. Combine the almond flour, Parmesan cheese, salt, basil, oregano, thyme, olive oil, and egg in a mixing bowl. The dough will be the consistency of cookie batter.

3. Spread the dough thinly on the prepared baking sheet by covering the dough with a piece of plastic wrap and patting it flat with your hands or rolling with a rolling pin to a 6- to 8-inch (15- to 20-cm) diameter.

4. Remove the plastic wrap.

5. Evenly lay the poached pear slices on the raw dough.

6. Top with the caramelized onions and slices of Gorgonzola cheese.

7. Bake until the cheese is melted and bubbly and the crust is brown around the edges, about 18 to 20 minutes.

8. Slice and serve hot from the oven.

½ cup (125 mL) **almond flour**

1 Tbsp (15 mL) grated **Parmesan cheese**

¼ tsp (1 mL) **salt**

½ tsp (2 mL) **dried basil**

½ tsp (2 mL) **dried oregano**

¼ tsp (1 mL) **dried thyme**

1 tsp (5 mL) **olive oil**

1 large **egg**

POACHED PEARS

CARAMELIZED ONIONS

¼ lb (125 g) **Gorgonzola cheese**, sliced

WARM PECAN-CRUSTED GOAT CHEESE ON ORGANIC GREENS

Serves 4

Oddly enough, every time I serve goat cheese and tell my guests that it is my homemade goat cheese, I get the exact same response: "You own a goat?" Maybe it's my friends; maybe it's human nature; but it's the same thing with different people *every time*—it's like a Seinfeld episode! I can't wait to hear what your friends say! But seriously, the creaminess of the warmed goat cheese inside the nutty, crunchy shell of the pecans is exquisite in this dish. Use a mixture of organic baby spinach and other young greens along with **CITRUS VINAIGRETTE** for this more delicate salad. —JB

1. Combine the pecan meal, salt, and freshly ground pepper in a shallow bowl.

2. In another shallow bowl, lightly beat the egg white with 1 tsp (5 mL) of water.

3. Slice the goat cheese into 12 pieces (see **SLICING GOAT CHEESE** on page 112).

4. Dip the goat cheese, 1 piece at a time, into the egg and then into the pecan meal, covering all sides.

5. Refrigerate the pecan-crusted rounds for 30 minutes.

6. Heat the olive oil in a medium-sized pan over medium heat.

7. When the oil is smoking, add the goat cheese and cook until the pecans are browned, but not burned. Flip and cook the second side and then remove from the pan.

8. Toss the salad greens with the dressing to taste and divide into 4 servings.

9. Evenly distribute the cheese over the dressed greens. Serve immediately.

½ cup (125 mL) **pecans**, chopped very finely into pecan meal

salt and freshly ground **black pepper** to taste

1 large **egg white**

1 tsp (5 mL) **water**

6 oz (175 g) **GOAT CHEESE** (page 31)

2 Tbsp (30 mL) **olive oil**

8 cups (2 L) **mixed organic field greens**

CITRUS VINAIGRETTE (page 91)

BABY SPINACH WITH GOAT CHEESE AND WARMED CITRUS VINAIGRETTE

Serves 4

I got this idea years ago from my friend Kimberly Gibson when she raved about a salad she served with a warmed salad dressing that melted the goat cheese and lightly wilted the lettuce. Top this delicious salad with either candied pecans or toasted pine nuts for a beautiful presentation. —JB

8 cups (2 L) **mixed organic field greens** or **baby spinach**, washed and dried well

6 oz (175 g) **GOAT CHEESE** (page 31), sliced (see **SLICING GOAT CHEESE** below)

½ cup (125 mL) **CANDIED PECANS** (page 45) or ¼ cup (60 mL) toasted **PINE NUTS** (see **TOASTING PINE NUTS** on page 92)

CITRUS VINAIGRETTE (page 91)

1. Put the spinach into a large salad bowl and add the goat cheese.

2. Warm the salad dressing on the stove or in the microwave for a few seconds—you want it warm, but not hot.

3. Pour the warmed dressing to taste over the salad and gently toss to combine.

4. Divide among the plates and top with the pecans or pine nuts.

5. Serve immediately.

SLICING GOAT CHEESE

The best way to slice goat cheese is to use a piece of thread or dental floss (unflavored!). Cut a piece of thread about 8 inches (20 cm) long. Wind the thread around your index fingers, holding it taught with your thumb as you would normally to floss your teeth. Slide the thread vertically through the log of goat cheese, slicing each piece as thick as you want it. The thread goes through the cheese better than a knife with no sticking and no mess.

THAI MANGO SALAD

Serves 2

Up until two years ago, I had never tried mango. I swear! I had assumed it was similar to papaya, a fruit that I had tried and definitely didn't like. When a friend finally made me try mango, it was love at first bite. Since then, it has become one of my favorite foods and I just cannot get enough. Top this mango salad with honey peanuts and tiny, dried shrimp, which you will find in Asian food markets. If your city has a Chinatown, you can certainly find them there. Although not necessary, both the salty shrimp and sweet honey peanuts round out the flavors and add authenticity to this Asian dish. Enjoy this easy, refreshing salad. It's cool and spicy, sweet and savory—perfect! —JB

1. Peel and slice the mango into thin slices and set aside in a bowl.

2. Combine the lime juice, honey, and chili flakes and pour over the mango. Toss to mix well.

3. Taste and season with salt and freshly ground pepper if necessary.

4. Refrigerate for 15 to 30 minutes to let the flavors blend.

5. Remove from the refrigerator and toss again.

6. Sprinkle with the shrimp and crushed honey peanuts and serve.

2 medium-sized **mangoes**, ripe but not too soft or overripe

juice of 1 **lime**

1 Tbsp (15 mL) **honey**

1 pinch of **hot chili flakes**

salt and freshly ground **black pepper** to taste

2 Tbsp (30 mL) **dried shrimp** (optional)

¼ cup (60 mL) **HONEY PEANUTS** (page 46), coarsely chopped (optional)

SIDES

CARAMELIZED ONION AND CELERY ROOT MASH

Serves 2

I first met Chef Robyn Goorevitch when I hired her to prepare a dinner for two to celebrate my husband Steven's 45th birthday. Robyn willingly accommodated my food restrictions and produced a feast that we still talk about. A few years later, I hired Robyn again to prepare dinner for six to celebrate my birthday (I'm not saying which one!). In between those two occasions, Robyn and I became friends and when I asked her if she would be willing to share any of her fabulous recipes with me, true to form, Robyn produced not one dish, but offered up an entire dinner! So this recipe is the first of it. Serve this dish as suggested in **CHEF ROBYN GOOREVITCH'S DINNER FOR TWO** on page 202 with **ROSEMARY AND MINT RACK OF LAMB** (page 160) and **BAKED HUBBARD SQUASH WITH HONEY AND CINNAMON** (page 126). —JB

1. Cut the onion in half and remove the skin. Slice the onion vertically as thin as possible into half moons.

2. Heat the butter and oil in a frying pan on medium heat and add the onion. Cook, stirring frequently for about 20 minutes, until the onion is soft and browned. If the pan dries out, add 1 Tbsp (15 mL) of water to prevent burning.

3. While the onion is cooking, peel and slice the celery root into 1-inch (2.5-cm) chunks.

4. Place the celery root in a large pot filled with cold water. Bring to a boil and cook on high heat until the celery root is tender, about 30 minutes.

5. Strain the celery root and mash it with a fork or potato masher. For a smoother mash, use an immersion blender.

6. Add the caramelized onions and mix.

7. Season with salt and freshly ground pepper. Serve warm.

1 **sweet onion** (try Vidalia onions when they are in season)

1 Tbsp (15 mL) **butter**

1 Tbsp (15 mL) **olive oil**

1 **celery root**

salt and freshly ground **black pepper** to taste

CAULIFLOWER MASH

Serves 4

This dish has become one of our favorites. It can be made ahead and reheated on the stove or in the microwave. Mashed cauliflower is a great substitute for mashed potatoes and goes well with just about everything. Follow steps 1 to 5 of this recipe when preparing the cauliflower for **CABBAGE ROLLS** (page 154).

1 large head of **cauliflower**

1 handful of **fresh chives**, chopped

1 Tbsp (15 mL) **butter** or more to taste

1 dash of **nutmeg**

salt and freshly ground **black pepper** to taste

1. Peel the leaves and green stem from the cauliflower, and coarsely chop the rest, including the white stems.

2. Steam the cauliflower in a large pot on high heat until the cauliflower is very soft, about 15 to 20 minutes.

3. Remove from the stove, drain the water from the pot, and let the cauliflower cool a bit until it is easier to handle.

4. When it's cool, place the cauliflower in a large dish towel, gather the ends, and wring the cauliflower of most of its water.

5. Mash the cauliflower with a fork or potato masher, or purée half or all of it using an immersion blender.

6. Season with the chopped chives, butter, nutmeg, salt, and freshly ground pepper.

7. Reheat if necessary and serve.

MUSHROOM "RISOTTO"

Serves 6 to 8

This is our colleague Fannie DeCaria's recipe. She taught Specific Carbohydrate Diet–cooking classes with us in Toronto and when she made this dish, we (and our students) were blown away. We felt as though we had rediscovered rice, a grain that most of us hadn't been able to eat for years. This mock risotto's delicate flavor makes it perfect for serving with almost any meal.

1. Soak the porcini mushrooms in the boiling water for 20 minutes. Drain, keeping the liquid and the mushrooms separate.

2. Pass the liquid through a fine sieve to strain out any small mushroom pieces. Reserve the liquid.

3. Chop the porcini mushrooms and set aside.

4. Grate the cauliflower using the shredding or grating blade of your food processor.

5. Bring a large pot of water to a boil and cook the grated cauliflower until tender, about 3 minutes. Drain using a sieve and rinse with cold water. Set aside.

6. Heat the olive oil in a large pan and cook the onion and garlic until softened but not brown.

7. Toss in the fresh mushrooms. Season with salt and freshly ground pepper and cook, stirring for 1 to 2 minutes.

8. Add the porcini mushrooms and the reserved cooking liquid, the wine, and the chicken stock. Increase the heat and cook until the liquid has been reduced by about half.

9. Add the cooked cauliflower and reduce the heat to low, stirring continuously until the stock has been absorbed—be careful not to overcook or the cauliflower will become too soft.

10. Remove from the heat, stir in the Parmesan cheese, and top with parsley.

5 dried **porcini mushrooms**

1 cup (250 mL) boiling **water**

½ head of **cauliflower**

2 Tbsp (30 mL) **olive oil**

1 or 2 small **onions**, finely chopped

1 **garlic clove**, crushed

2 cups (500 mL) fresh **mushrooms**, sliced

salt and freshly ground **black pepper** to taste

2 Tbsp (30 mL) **CHICKEN STOCK** (page 44)

2 Tbsp (30 mL) **dry white wine**

2 Tbsp (30 mL) or to taste grated **Parmesan cheese**

3 Tbsp (45 mL) finely chopped **fresh parsley**

CURRY "RISOTTO"

Serves 6 to 8

Whether or not you are able to eat rice, we guarantee you will love this mock risotto recipe, which is a fusion of Thai and Indian curry flavors. Our colleague Fannie DeCaria developed this rice substitute technique based on a suggestion in *15-Minute Low-Carb Recipes* by Dana Carpenter—try Fannie's original **MUSHROOM "RISOTTO"** on page 117.

1. Grate the cauliflower using the shredding or grating blade of your food processor.

2. Place the grated cauliflower in a pot and cover with water. Bring it to a boil and cook for 3 minutes. Drain using a sieve and rinse the cauliflower with cold water. Set aside.

3. Heat the butter in a large pan.

4. Add the onion, garlic, and green beans, and sauté on medium heat for 6 to 8 minutes.

5. Add the rest of the ingredients and stir until the sauce is mixed well and heated through.

6. Turn the heat down to low and add the cauliflower. Stir until thoroughly combined.

7. Serve hot.

½ head of **cauliflower**

3 Tbsp (45 mL) **butter**

2 **garlic cloves**, crushed

1 medium **onion**, finely diced

1 cup (250 mL) **string beans**, coarsely chopped

¼ cup (60 mL) **water**

¼ cup (60 mL) **YOGURT** (page 27)

¼ cup (60 mL) **TOMATO PASTE** (page 42)

2 Tbsp (30 mL) **cashew butter**

1 Tbsp (15 mL) **honey**

½ tsp (2 mL) mild, medium, or hot **curry powder**

½ tsp (2 mL) ground **cinnamon**

1 pinch of **cayenne pepper**

1 pinch of **salt**

FIVE MUSHROOM BAKE
Serves 4

Wonderful and cheesy and super easy—that's the best way to describe this mushroom casserole. This dish can even be assembled ahead of time and baked just before serving.

1 tsp (5 mL) **olive oil**

1 lb (500 g) combination of fresh **Portobello**, **white**, **oyster**, **cremini**, and **shiitake mushrooms**, coarsely chopped

3 tsp (15 mL) **butter**, divided

salt and freshly ground **black pepper** to taste

2 oz (60 g) combination of grated **Parmesan** and **cheddar cheeses**

1. Preheat the oven to 400°F (200°C).

2. Heat the olive oil and 2 tsp (10 mL) of the butter in a large pot over medium heat and add the mushrooms.

3. Stir frequently while they cook through, about 5 to 7 minutes.

4. If there is a lot of liquid at the bottom of the pan, increase the heat to high and continue to stir until the liquid evaporates.

5. When the liquid has evaporated, stir in the remaining 1 tsp (5 mL) of butter, salt, and freshly ground pepper.

6. Pour the entire mixture into a small casserole dish and top with the cheese.

7. Bake until the cheese bubbles, about 15 minutes. Serve hot.

ZUCCHINI FRIES

Serves 4

Who doesn't like fried foods? Sure, they may not be all that healthy, but every now and then it's fun to indulge. Something about frying makes anything taste good—I always say you could fry shoelaces and they'd taste great! Serve these fries as a side dish or fry up a batch and serve them as an hors d'oeuvre for company with **AIOLI** (page 35) as a dipping sauce. For a more heart-healthy breaded vegetable side dish, see **BAKED ONION AND BELL PEPPER RINGS** on page 122. –JB

1. Slice the zucchini into French fry–sized slices.

2. Cover the bottom of a frying pan with a ½-inch (1-cm) layer of oil and heat over medium-high heat until hot but not smoking.

3. Lightly beat the eggs in a shallow bowl.

4. Mix the grated Parmesan cheese, salt, and cayenne pepper in another shallow bowl until well combined.

5. Dip the zucchini pieces into the beaten egg, give them a shake to remove excess egg, and then roll them in the Parmesan cheese mixture.

6. Carefully place the "fries" in the oil and fry until cooked through and lightly browned, about 2 to 3 minutes.

7. Drain on paper towels.

8. Serve hot.

peanut oil for frying

1 lb (500 g) **zucchini**, peeled

2 large **eggs**, beaten

finely grated **Parmesan cheese** to taste

1 tsp (5 mL) **salt**

¼ tsp (1 mL) **cayenne pepper**

BAKED ONION AND BELL PEPPER RINGS

Serves 6 to 8

Here is a more heart-healthy breaded vegetable variation. These savory baked onion and bell pepper rings stray from tradition, but they taste just as sinful as their fried counterparts.

2 large **eggs**

1 Tbsp (15 mL) **Dijon mustard**

2 cups (500 mL) **almond flour**

¼ cup (60 mL) grated **Parmesan cheese**

¼ tsp (1 mL) **cayenne pepper**

½ tsp (2 mL) **salt**

1 **sweet onion** (try Vidalia onions when they are in season), sliced into rings

1 **red**, **green**, or **yellow bell pepper**, sliced into rings

olive oil for drizzling

1. Preheat the oven to 375°F (190°C) and line a baking sheet with parchment paper.

2. Combine the eggs and mustard in a bowl and mix well.

3. In another bowl, mix the almond flour, Parmesan, cayenne pepper, and salt.

4. Toss the onion and bell pepper rings in the egg mixture until they are thoroughly coated.

5. Toss the vegetables in the flour mixture until they are thoroughly coated.

6. Spread the coated vegetables evenly on the prepared baking sheet and drizzle with olive oil.

7. Bake until the vegetables are soft and the breading is golden brown, about 15 to 20 minutes.

8. Serve hot.

DIJON BUNS

Makes 12 buns

These savory, tangy buns are great at dinner, for a snack, or to accompany a salad for lunch. Serve them hot with butter.

1. Preheat the oven to 325°F (160°C) and line a baking sheet with parchment paper.

2. Combine the almond flour, baking soda, and cayenne pepper in a bowl and mix well.

3. In another bowl, combine the dill, mustard, garlic, and eggs and mix well.

4. Add the flour mixture to the egg mixture and stir until well blended.

5. Divide the dough into 12 buns and place them evenly on the prepared baking sheet.

6. Bake until the buns begin to brown, about 18 to 20 minutes.

2½ cups (625 mL) **almond flour**

½ tsp (2 mL) **baking soda**

¼ to ½ tsp (1 to 2 mL) **cayenne pepper**

¼ cup (60 mL) chopped **fresh dill**

¼ cup (60 mL) **Dijon mustard**

1 **garlic clove**, crushed

3 large **eggs**

CARROT AND APPLE KUGEL

Serves 4

A *kugel* (pronounced kOO-gul) is the Yiddish word for baked pudding. Although typically savory and made from potatoes or noodles, they are now just as commonly made sweet with vegetables and fruit. Enjoy this delicious sweet kugel as a side dish with chicken or turkey, and reheat leftovers for breakfast the next morning.

2 cups (500 mL) grated **carrot**

1 cup (250 mL) grated **apple**

2 large **eggs**

⅓ cup (75 mL) **honey**

1 Tbsp (15 mL) freshly squeezed **lemon juice**

2 cups (500 mL) **almond flour**

1 tsp (5 mL) **baking soda**

½ tsp (2 mL) **salt**

1. Preheat the oven to 350°F (180°C) and line a 9- x 5-inch (2-L) loaf pan with parchment paper.

2. Combine the carrot, apple, eggs, honey, and lemon juice in a large bowl.

3. In another bowl, combine the almond flour, baking soda, and salt.

4. Add the dry ingredients to the wet and mix thoroughly.

5. Pour the mixture into the prepared pan and bake until a knife inserted in the middle comes out clean, about 35 to 45 minutes.

6. Let the kugel cool for a few minutes before removing it from the loaf pan.

7. Slice and serve warm.

SWEET SQUASH KUGEL
Serves 6 to 8

When I was growing up, kugel was one of my favorite foods (see page 124 for a definition of "kugel"). My family usually made a sweet noodle kugel with raisins and margarine and, after I stopped being able to eat grains, I could only watch with envy as everyone around me indulged in this treat during holiday dinners. But when I was faced with teaching a Specific Carbohydrate Diet holiday cooking class in 2006, I decided to recreate a version of my beloved kugel that would be legal for the SCD. This sweet kugel uses spaghetti squash instead of noodles and according my family, you would never know the difference. —JL

1. Preheat the oven to 350°F (180°C) and grease an 8-inch (2-L) square casserole dish.

2. Mix the honey, butter, cheese, vanilla, eggs, raisins, and squash in a bowl.

3. Pour the batter into the prepared casserole dish and sprinkle the top with cinnamon.

4. Bake until set, about 50 to 60 minutes.

¼ cup (60 mL) **honey**

3 Tbsp (45 mL) **butter**

¼ cup (60 mL) **YOGURT CHEESE** (page 28)

1 Tbsp (15 mL) **PURE VANILLA EXTRACT** (page 36)

3 large **eggs**

¼ to ½ cup (60 to 125 mL) **raisins**

3 to 4 cups (750 mL to 1 L) cooked **SPAGHETTI SQUASH** (page 43)

ground **cinnamon** for sprinkling

BAKED HUBBARD SQUASH WITH HONEY AND CINNAMON

Serves 2

Hubbard squash is a seasonal squash available between September and March. It comes with either a green or orange skin, and is neither as sweet as butternut squash nor as dry as buttercup squash. If you cannot find Hubbard squash, you can use acorn, pepper, or any winter squash instead. This is the second dish of the dinner trio offered by Personal Chef Robyn Goorevitch, which includes **ROSEMARY AND MINT RACK OF LAMB** (page 160) and **CARAMELIZED ONION AND CELERY ROOT MASH** (page 115).

½ **Hubbard squash**, seeds removed and cut into ½-inch (1-cm) strips

1 Tbsp (15 mL) **honey**

1 tsp (5 mL) ground **cinnamon**

1. Preheat the oven to 400°F (200°C) and line a baking sheet with parchment paper.

2. Place the strips of Hubbard squash on the prepared baking sheet.

3. Mix the honey with the cinnamon and, using a pastry brush, brush the surface of the squash with the mixture.

4. Roast until golden brown, about 45 minutes.

CANDY BEETS

Serves 4

"Try it. They taste like candy!" That's what my grandmother used to tell my mother whenever she wanted her to try new food. I'm sure this was not always the truth, but if my grandmother had said it about this dish, it would not have been a lie. If you aren't a fan of beets (as I was not), this dish from my friend Gillian Marshall will change your mind … try it, it tastes like candy! —JB

1. Preheat the oven to 350°F (180°C) and line a baking sheet with parchment paper.

2. Wash and peel the beets, and cut them into chunks.

3. Place the beets in a bowl and toss them with olive oil.

4. Place them on the prepared baking sheet and bake, turning frequently until cooked through and caramelized, about 45 to 60 minutes.

5. Remove from the oven and sprinkle with salt and freshly ground pepper if desired.

6 **beets**

olive oil

salt and freshly ground **black pepper** (optional)

MANGO SALSA
Makes 2 cups (500 mL)

It seems that everywhere you look these days, no matter what the season, you can find beautiful mangoes. Mangoes are wonderfully versatile; they work well as a salad, side dish, or accompaniment to any number of proteins, and are perfect for dessert. In this salsa, the mango's cool, tangy sweetness works well with the hot spiciness of the jalapeno pepper and onions. Enjoy this salsa as a side dish with any meal or use it as a chutney served over **DRY-RUB SALMON BARBECUED ON A CEDAR PLANK** (page 142).

1 medium-sized firm and not over-ripe **mango**, chopped

½ cup (125 mL) chopped **red bell pepper**

¼ cup (60 mL) finely chopped **red onion**

1½ tsp (7 mL) finely chopped **jalapeno pepper**, seeds removed

2 Tbsp (30 mL) finely chopped **Italian parsley**

juice of 1 **lime**

1. Combine all the ingredients in a bowl and stir.

2. Refrigerate for a couple of hours to let the flavors combine and serve.

PINEAPPLE MARMALADE

Makes 3 cups (750 mL)

This is the second recipe that Chef Christopher Ennew at Ste. Anne's Spa wanted us to share with you (see his smoothie recipe on page 69). Chef Ennew recommends using this marmalade to top fish. Try it with **DRY-RUB SALMON BARBECUED ON A CEDAR PLANK** (page 142).

1. Heat the honey in a medium-sized pot.

2. Add the grapefruit slices and cook on medium heat until transparent, about 10 minutes.

3. Stir in the pineapple and cook for 2 more minutes.

4. Let cool. Fold in the cardamom and fresh herbs and serve.

½ cup (125 mL) **honey**

1 medium-sized **pink grapefruit**, cut into 8 thinly sliced wedges

1 whole **golden pineapple**, cleaned and diced into small pieces

1 pinch of ground **cardamom**

¼ bunch **fresh parsley**, finely chopped

⅛ bunch **fresh cilantro**, finely chopped

SIMPLE VEGETABLE SIDES

Sometimes you just want ideas for simple vegetable side dishes that are healthy and work with just about any main course. Here are some quick veggie sides that work for everyday meals or for company.

STEAMED GREEN BEANS

1. Wash and snip the ends off the beans.

2. Steam until just tender, about 3 to 5 minutes.

3. Drizzle with melted butter and season with salt and freshly ground pepper to taste.

4. Garnish with sliced or slivered almonds and serve.

GRILLED ASPARAGUS

1. Wash and snap the woody ends off the asparagus.

2. Toss with a bit of oil and salt.

3. Grill on the barbecue over medium-high heat, turning frequently until they are browned and their natural sugars have caramelized. Serve warm.

SNOW PEAS AND SNAP PEAS

1. Wash and cut the ends off the pods.

2. Place in a frying pan with just enough water to cover the bottom of the pan and steam until just tender, about 2 to 3 minutes. Drain.

3. Return the peas to the pan and sauté with a bit of butter, salt, and freshly ground pepper to taste.

4. Sprinkle with sesame seeds and serve.

SAUTÉED MUSHROOMS

1. Chop assorted mushrooms into equal-sized pieces.

2. Sauté the mushrooms in a frying pan on medium heat with a bit of butter.

3. When cooked through and the moisture has evaporated, season with salt and freshly ground pepper before serving.

BAKED CAULIFLOWER

1. Preheat the oven to 400°F (200°C) and line a baking sheet with parchment paper.

2. Separate the cauliflower into florets.

3. Toss the florets in a bowl with a bit of olive oil.

4. Place them on the prepared baking sheet and sprinkle liberally with salt.

5. Roast until browned to your liking, about 45 minutes.

STEAMED BROCCOLI

1. Slice the broccoli by following the line of the florets all the way down the stalk.

2. Steam in a vegetable steamer or in a large frying pan with just enough water to cover the bottom until bright green and just tender.

3. Serve with a pat of butter and season with salt and freshly ground pepper to taste.

continued on next page

CARAMELIZED CARROTS

1. Peel and slice carrots into long, thin strips.

2. Toss the carrots in some olive oil, salt, freshly ground black pepper, and paprika.

3. Sauté the carrots over medium heat in more olive oil until they start to soften and brown or blacken, about 7 to 10 minutes.

SIMPLE SALAD

1. Chop several romaine lettuce hearts.

2. Add sunflower seeds and Parmesan cheese.

3. Toss with your favorite dressing or any of our salad dressings (pages 89 to 92).

SLICED TOMATOES WITH GOAT CHEESE

1. Slice several ripe tomatoes into ¼-inch (5-mm) slices and arrange them on a decorative serving plate.

2. Sprinkle with crumbled **GOAT CHEESE** (page 31) and chopped fresh basil.

3. Drizzle with olive oil and red wine vinegar, and sprinkle with salt and freshly ground pepper.

MAINS

CANNELLONI

Serves 6

Our friend and colleague Carol Frilegh developed this cannelloni dish, which tastes like the real deal. Whenever she makes it, I can't help but indulge, even though I have a sensitivity to provolone cheese. Carol's cannelloni is just too good to pass up. Follow her egg crêpe recipe or use **BASIC CRÊPES** (page 48) if you have some on hand. —JL

TOMATO SAUCE

1. Brown the onions and garlic in the olive oil in a large pan.

2. Remove the onions and garlic from the pan and set aside.

3. Brown the meat in the same pan used to cook the onions and garlic. Drain the fat if desired.

4. Return the onions and garlic to the pan along with the meat, tomato juice, tomatoes (if desired), bay leaf, and oregano. Cook uncovered until the sauce reaches the desired thickness, at least 1 hour.

5. Add salt and freshly ground pepper to taste.

1 Tbsp (15 mL) **olive oil**

1 large **onion**, minced

1 to 2 **garlic cloves**, minced

1 lb (500 g) **lean ground beef**

one 48-oz (1.36-L) can of **tomato juice**

3 to 4 **fresh tomatoes**, coarsely chopped (optional)

1 **bay leaf**

½ to 1 tsp (2 to 5 mL) **dried oregano**

salt and freshly ground **black pepper**

EGG CRÊPES

1. Place a cloth dish towel on the countertop.

2. Heat the butter or oil in a small pan.

3. Beat the eggs with a few drops of water.

4. Pour ¼ cup (60 mL) of the beaten egg into the pan and gently tilt it to distribute the egg evenly.

butter or **oil** for cooking

3 to 4 large **eggs**

few drops of **water**

continued on next page

5. Cook until the egg is set but still slightly moist on top. Carefully remove the egg crêpe with a spatula and flip it onto the dish towel, top side down. Let cool.

6. Repeat with the rest of the batter.

FILLING AND ASSEMBLY

2 large **eggs**

¼ cup (60 mL) **dry-curd cottage cheese**

½ lb (250 g) grated **provolone cheese** for filling, plus ¼ cup (60 mL) for topping

½ cup (125 mL) grated **Parmesan cheese**

1 tsp (5 mL) chopped **parsley**

1 pinch of ground **cinnamon**

1. Preheat the oven to 350°F (180°C).

2. Beat the eggs with a fork and mix in the remaining ingredients.

3. Divide the filling evenly among the crêpes and roll.

4. Place half the tomato sauce in a casserole dish and place the rolled crêpes in the dish with space between them.

5. Cover the rolled crêpes with the rest of the sauce and top with the remaining ¼ cup (60 mL) grated provolone cheese.

6. Bake for 30 minutes, until heated through.

7. Cool for 10 minutes before serving.

SPINACH GNOCCHI

Makes 48 pieces

Inspired by the gnocchi at Imperia, a restaurant in Toronto's Yorkville area that is owned by my friend Franco Agostino, this dish is made legal for the Specific Carbohydrate Diet by using homemade goat cheese rather than ricotta. Franco was generous enough to invite me into his restaurant's kitchen to work with Chef Christopher Palik to learn how to make these little dumplings using my grain-free restrictions. What follows is a combination of their suggestions and my instinct. The result is a delicious treat that makes a wonderful main course or a perfect prelude to a meal. These gnocchi, served in a sage-butter sauce and garnished with Parmesan cheese, can be prepared ahead of time and refrigerated until ready to cook and serve. —JB

GNOCCHI

1. Drain the blanched spinach—first by squeezing it in your hands in small batches and then by rolling it in a dish towel and ringing out all its moisture.

2. Place the dried spinach in your food processor and add the egg yolks. Process until smooth.

3. Add the goat cheese, Parmesan cheese, nutmeg, salt, and freshly ground pepper to taste. Process again until smooth.

4. Transfer to a bowl and mix in the almond flour. Refrigerate for 30 minutes to 1 hour to make the dough easier to handle.

5. Remove from the refrigerator and form the dough into small oval shapes, about the size of an olive. At this point, they can be returned to the refrigerator until you are ready to prepare them or you can proceed with the assembly.

1 lb (500 g) **fresh baby spinach**, blanched (see **BLANCHING SPINACH** on page 139)

3 large **egg yolks**

¼ lb (125 g) **GOAT CHEESE** (page 31)

1½ oz (45 g) grated **Parmesan cheese**

¼ tsp (1 mL) **nutmeg**

salt and freshly ground **black pepper** to taste

½ cup (125 mL) finely ground **almond flour** (see **FINELY GROUND ALMOND FLOUR** on page 54)

continued on next page

SAGE BUTTER SAUCE AND ASSEMBLY

1. Bring a large pot of water to a boil. While waiting for the water to boil, prepare the sage butter sauce.

2. Gently heat the sage and the butter in a small frying pan on low and warm until the butter is melted. Add salt to taste.

3. Keep warm on very low heat.

4. Add the gnocchi to the boiling water in 2 batches—they will sink at first and then rise to the top when they are cooked.

5. Carefully remove the gnocchi from the pot of boiling water with a slotted spoon, blotting the excess water by touching the bottom of the spoon to a dish cloth or paper towel.

6. Carefully transfer the gnocchi to the frying pan and evenly coat them with the sage butter sauce by giving them a gentle swirl in the pan.

7. Gently transfer the gnocchi into serving bowls and sprinkle with a bit of grated Parmesan cheese before serving.

¼ cup (60 mL) **unsalted butter**

10 **sage leaves**, torn

salt to taste

freshly grated **Parmesan cheese** for garnishing

BLANCHING SPINACH

Blanching is a simple technique used to lightly cook vegetables while preserving their color, texture, and flavor. Here's what to do:

1. Bring a large pot of water to a rapid boil.

2. While the water heats, take a large bowl and fill it halfway with ice. Add cold water until the ice reaches three-quarters of the way up the side of the bowl.

3. When the water in the pot boils, add the spinach.

4. Remove the spinach when it is thoroughly wilted and bright green, about 30 seconds.

5. Plunge the spinach quickly into the ice water to stop the cooking process and to preserve its bright green color. Cool the spinach in the ice water and then remove.

PORTUGUESE BACALHAU (SALT COD)

Serves 4

Bacalhau or salt cod is a standard in Portuguese restaurants, and it is said that there are as many ways to prepare salt cod as there are days of the year. This method is our favorite: baked and served with caramelized sweet onions. Salt cod can often be found in the freezer section of your grocery store. If you cannot find it there, ask your fish monger. Salt cod must be soaked for 24 to 48 hours to remove the salt used to preserve it, so this dish certainly isn't one you can put together at the last minute. But it's good enough to be worth the forethought!

SOAKING THE COD

2 lb (1 kg) **salt cod**

water for soaking

1. Arrange the salt cod in a single layer in a 9- x 13-inch (3.5-L) casserole dish.

2. Cover it with water and refrigerate for 24 to 48 hours.

3. Change the water occasionally (3 to 4 times).

BAKING AND ASSEMBLY

olive oil for cooking the onion, plus 2 Tbsp (30 mL) olive oil for cooking the garlic

2 large **sweet onions**, thinly sliced

3 **garlic cloves**, pressed

lemon wedges for garnish

1. Pan fry the onions with a little olive oil in a large frying pan over medium heat for about 20 minutes, until they are soft and browned. If the pan dries out, add 1 Tbsp (15 mL) of water to prevent burning.

2. Remove the onions from the pan and let them cool.

3. Preheat the oven to 450°F (230°C).

4. Drain the water from the salt cod and pat it dry. Dry the casserole dish as well.

5. Arrange the cod in a single layer in the dish it was soaking in.

6. Heat the 2 Tbsp (30 mL) of olive oil on low and add the garlic. Cook lightly until the garlic is fragrant, about 10 to 20 seconds. Don't let the garlic brown or it will be bitter.

7. Brush the fish with the olive oil and garlic mixture.

8. Bake the fish in the oven on the second highest rack for 15 minutes.

9. Remove from the oven and cover the fish with the caramelized onions. Return to the oven and bake until the fish is done and the onions are warmed through, about 5 more minutes.

10. Serve with lemon wedges.

DRY-RUB SALMON BARBECUED ON A CEDAR PLANK

Serves 4

When you barbecue food on a cedar plank, you impart its subtle smokiness to whatever you are cooking, while the moisture from the pre-soaked plank helps to steam the food and keep it moist. Cedar planks are available in grocery stores and are inexpensive. This cedar-plank barbecued salmon is seasoned with a dry rub, which is quite literally a mixture of dry herbs and spices that you rub on meat, fowl, or fish. Dry rubs are supposed to be intensely flavorful and this one is no exception. For another dry-rub blend, see **DRY-RUB STEAK SPICE** (page 165). Try serving this salmon topped with **PINEAPPLE MARMALADE** (page 129) or **MANGO SALSA** (page 128)—even though the salsa also has a bit of a kick, it complements the dish by adding a cool, sweetness to the spiciness of the salmon.

1 or 2 **cedar planks** large enough to hold 4 salmon fillets

2 Tbsp (30 mL) **Spanish paprika**

1 Tbsp (15 mL) **salt**

½ tsp (2 mL) cracked **black pepper**

¼ tsp (1 mL) ground **cinnamon**

¼ tsp (1 mL) **cayenne pepper**

4 **salmon fillets**

1. Soak your cedar plank in water for at least 6 hours.

2. To make the dry rub, combine the paprika, salt, cracked pepper, cinnamon, and cayenne pepper in a bowl and mix.

3. Divide the spice mixture evenly among the 4 pieces of salmon and rub into the top, bottom, and sides of the fish. If the skin is still on the salmon, rub the spices into the skin.

4. Refrigerate for at least 2 hours and up to 6 hours.

5. Preheat the barbecue to high.

6. Shake the water off the cedar planks.

7. Place the salmon fillets on the planks, skin side down.

8. Place the planks on the barbecue and grill with indirect heat by reducing the heat to low under the grilling side and turning the side not in use to high.

9. Cover the barbecue.

10. Cook for 10 to 15 minutes. Turn the fish over and barbecue the second side for the last 5 minutes of cooking time.

11. Remove the fish from the planks and serve.

12. When cool, dispose of the planks. They can only be used once.

SPICY PEEL-AND-EAT SHRIMP

Serves 4

Shrimp, like eggs, were once considered unhealthy due to their high cholesterol content. However, we now know that shrimp are as healthy as they are delicious. Studies show that the cholesterol in shrimp doesn't adversely affect blood cholesterol levels, and that they are very low in calories and saturated fat (see **BAD FAT** on page 16). Another reason to eat shrimp is their excellent nutrition—they are high in vitamins D and B12, and are a source of DHA, the "good" fat that nourishes the brain (see **GOOD FAT** on page 15). So we are pleased to bring you this quick, easy, delicious—and nutritious—shrimp recipe. You will be licking your fingers and fighting over every last shrimp in this dish!

1. Thaw the shrimp according to the instructions on the package.

2. When thawed, rinse thoroughly with water and drain.

3. Coat a large frying pan or wok with sunflower oil and turn the heat to high.

4. When the pan is hot, add the shrimp and stir.

5. Cook the shrimp half way, until they are starting to turn opaque, and remove them from the pan.

6. Add the green onions, garlic, and ginger to the pan and stir for 1 minute until fragrant. Return the shrimp to the pan and stir to coat completely with the garlic mixture.

7. Add the cayenne pepper, hot chili flakes, and salt and combine.

8. Continue to cook until the shrimp are opaque and just cooked through, about 2 to 3 minutes. Do not overcook.

9. Remove from the heat and serve hot.

2 lb (1 kg) **frozen large shrimp**, deveined, but with the skin and tail still on

1 Tbsp (15 mL) **sunflower oil**

6 **green onions** (white parts only), thinly sliced into threads

6 **garlic cloves**, minced

3 Tbsp (45 mL) **ginger**, grated

1 pinch of **cayenne pepper**

1 pinch of **hot pepper flakes**

1 tsp (5 mL) **salt**

SEARED TUNA WITH CARROT FRITTERS

Serves 4

Perfect for company, this dish is simple to make and looks beautiful. It is sure to please all the seared tuna lovers you know. The carrot fritters can be made ahead of time and reheated in a 250°F (120°C) oven for 30 minutes until hot. Serve with **AIOLI** (page 35).

FRITTERS

Makes about 16 fritters

1. Add the carrots, cheddar cheese, almond flour, and baking soda to a medium-sized bowl and toss to mix thoroughly.

2. In another small bowl, combine the eggs, mustard, yogurt, salt, and freshly ground pepper and stir well.

3. Add the dry ingredients to the wet and mix thoroughly.

4. Coat a frying pan with a bit of oil and turn to medium heat. It is not necessary to fry these fritters in a lot of oil; just a light coating of oil in the frying pan will do the job well.

5. Drop heaping **teaspoons** full of the mixture on the hot pan and fry, turning once, until browned and cooked through.

6. Place the cooked fritters on paper towels to absorb any excess oil. Transfer them to an ovenproof dish and keep them warm in the oven at 175°F (85°C).

1 cup (250 mL) grated **carrot**

½ cup (125 mL) grated **extra old cheddar cheese**

½ cup (125 mL) **almond flour**

1 tsp (5 mL) **baking soda**

2 large **eggs**

1 tsp (5 mL) **Dijon** or **seedy mustard**

¼ cup (60 mL) **YOGURT** (page 27)

1 pinch of **salt**

freshly ground **black pepper**

sunflower oil for cooking

SEARED TUNA

1. Brush the tuna with a bit of olive oil and season with salt and freshly ground pepper.

2. Heat a frying pan to smoking or heat a barbecue grill to high.

olive oil for brushing on the tuna

1½ lb (750 g) **sushi grade tuna**

salt and freshly ground **black pepper**

continued on next page

3. Sear the tuna in the pan or on the grill for 2 to 3 minutes per side, depending on the thickness of the fish.

4. Remove the tuna from the heat and let rest for 1 minute before slicing with the grain.

PLATING

AIOLI (page 35)

1. Remove the fritters from the warming oven.

2. Place one fritter on a dinner plate and add a dollop of aioli on top.

3. Cover the fritter with slices of the tuna.

4. Decorate the top of the tuna with more aioli and prop the second fritter up against the side of this tower.

5. Repeat steps 2 to 4 with the rest of the fritters.

6. Serve.

FRENCH ONION SOUP

Serves 4

We know your first question: "If you can't use French bread, what keeps the cheese afloat?" The answer: read and you shall see! Traditionally made with French bread to float the cheese, flour to thicken the broth, and, often, canned beef stock to flavor, this French onion soup calls for none of these starch sources. The use of lighter tasting homemade chicken stock allows the natural sweetness of the onions to come through. The sheer number of onions thickens the broth and, more importantly, fills the bowl. Finally, the addition of a whisked egg helps to keep the cheese afloat. Enjoy this hearty soup as part of a simple soup-and-salad dinner.

1. Peel and slice the onions. If you have a food processor, don't be a martyr! Use the coarse slicer attachment for this task—it will save a lot of time and stinging tears.

2. Melt the butter with the olive oil in a large pot over medium heat.

3. When the butter is melted and the oil and butter are sizzling, add the onions and garlic, and stir until the onions have softened, about 5 to 10 minutes.

4. Add the chicken broth and white wine and let the soup come to a slow boil.

5. Boil slowly for 15 minutes, stirring occasionally.

6. Cover and let simmer slowly for 30 minutes, stirring occasionally. You want the soup to cook, but you want as little water to evaporate as possible.

7. After 30 minutes, taste the soup and season with salt and freshly ground pepper as necessary.

8. Preheat the oven to 450°F (230°C).

9. Evenly divide the soup among 4 oven-safe bowls and whisk 1 egg into each.

10. Sprinkle the cheese on top of each bowl and turn the oven to broil. Set the bowls in the oven on a high rack. Broil until the cheese is browned to your liking.

11. Remove and serve hot.

2 lb (1 kg) **yellow cooking onions**

2 Tbsp (30 mL) **butter**

2 Tbsp (30 mL) **olive oil**

4 **garlic cloves**, minced

5 cups (1.25 L) **CHICKEN STOCK** (page 44)

1½ cups (375 mL) **dry white wine**

salt and freshly ground **black pepper** to taste

4 large **eggs**

¼ lb (125 g) **Gruyère cheese**, grated

¼ lb (125 g) **Swiss Emmenthal cheese**, grated

OPEN-FACED CHICKEN POT PIE

Serves 6 to 8

Chicken pot pie is comfort food at its best. This recipe combines a savory almond-flour pie crust with a rich chicken stew. It also freezes and reheats well. Note that if you choose to use more heart-healthy chicken breasts, the stew will be a bit less rich.

CRUST

3 cups (750 mL) **almond flour**

¾ tsp (4 mL) **salt**

¼ tsp (1 mL) **baking soda**

⅓ cup (75 mL) **butter**, melted

1 large **egg**

1. Preheat the oven to 300°F (150°C).

2. Mix the flour, salt, and baking soda in a bowl.

3. Add the butter and egg to the flour mixture and combine. The mixture will be crumbly, but continue to knead the dough until it forms a ball.

4. Press the dough into a 9-inch (23-cm) or 10-inch (25-cm) pie plate (this is enough dough to fit either size). Wet your hands with water to help make pressing and spreading the dough easier.

5. Bake until lightly browned, about 20 minutes.

6. Remove from the oven and let cool.

CHICKEN FILLING

1. Put the all the ingredients, except the peas, in a large pot, and add enough water to almost cover the contents.

2. With the lid on, bring to a medium boil over medium-high heat.

3. Reduce the heat to medium and cook with the lid ajar for 30 minutes, stirring occasionally.

4. Remove the lid and increase the heat to medium-high. Cook, stirring occasionally, until the stew bubbles vigorously and the sauce reduces and thickens, about 40 to 50 more minutes.

5. Add the peas and stir to mix them in well. Cook for about 2 more minutes, until the peas are heated through.

6. Turn off the heat, move the pot of stew to a cool burner, and let it sit for about 5 minutes.

ASSEMBLY

1. **To eat immediately**, pour the filling into the pie crust and serve hot. **To divide and freeze**, pour the filling into the pie crust and refrigerate for 2 hours. Cut the pie into 6 to 8 pieces and freeze each piece in an individual container.

2. Freeze any leftover filling to eat as a stew or use as the filling for another chicken pot pie.

1 lb (500 g) **boneless, skinless chicken thighs** or **breasts** cut into 1-inch (2.5 cm) pieces

½ **butternut squash**, peeled and diced, or 2 medium-sized **zucchinis**, diced

½ large **sweet onion** (try Vidalia onions when they are in season), diced

2 large **carrots**, peeled and diced

½ cup (125 mL) **YOGURT** (page 27) or **YOGURT CHEESE** (page 28)

1¼ tsp (6 mL) **salt**

¼ tsp (1 mL) freshly ground **black pepper**

1 cup (250 mL) fresh or frozen **peas**

CRISPY SOUTHERN CHICKEN
Serves 6 to 8

I could never stand eating plain chicken as a child (I still can't). So you can imagine my excitement the day my parents started using Coat 'n Bake (the kosher version of Shake 'n Bake). As a tribute to many happy Friday night meals, I've created my own version of breaded chicken based on a traditional Southern recipe. This dish can be made spicier by adding more freshly ground black pepper, cayenne pepper, or both. I've provided fried and baked options, but I prefer baked because the chicken is guaranteed to be crispy on the outside, juicy on the inside. —JL

FRIED OPTION

1. Mix the almond flour, salt, paprika, thyme, freshly ground pepper, and cayenne pepper.

2. Add the Dijon mustard to the beaten eggs and mix well.

3. Dredge the chicken pieces in the egg mixture and then in the flour mixture. Place the coated chicken in a 9- x 13-inch (3.5-L) casserole dish.

4. Add a ¼-inch (5-mm) layer of oil to a large frying pan and heat on medium-high heat until the oil is very hot.

5. Place several pieces of chicken in the oil at a time and cook for 2 minutes on each side. Put the fried chicken back in the casserole dish.

6. As you start frying your last batch of chicken, preheat the oven to 400°F (200°C).

7. Place the casserole dish in the oven and bake the chicken until cooked through, about 30 to 40 minutes.

2 cups (500 mL) **almond flour**

1 Tbsp (15 mL) **salt**

1 Tbsp (15 mL) **paprika**

1 Tbsp (15 mL) **dried thyme**

1 tsp (5 mL) freshly ground **black pepper**

1 tsp (5 mL) ground **cayenne pepper**

2 Tbsp (30 mL) **Dijon mustard**

2 large **eggs**, beaten

3 lb (1.5 kg) **chicken pieces**

olive oil (for fried option)

BAKED OPTION

1. Preheat the oven to 350°F (180°C).

2. Follow steps 1 to 3 in the fried option instructions.

3. Drizzle the chicken lightly with olive oil and bake until cooked through, about 75 to 80 minutes.

ITALIAN CHICKEN

Serves 6 to 8

I'm not a huge fan of lamb, but when Jodi invited me over to try a new lamb recipe, how could I refuse? It was delicious and I took a quick mental note of the ingredient list before I left that evening. I didn't quite remember everything, but I managed to improvise this simple chicken dish based on what I had tasted. It's no-fail and comes out tender and juicy every time—the meat literally falls off the bone. If you don't follow the Specific Carbohydrate Diet or your symptoms are in remission, feel free to use one 28-oz (796-mL) can of plum tomatoes with juice instead of the peeled plum tomatoes and tomato juice. —JL

3 lb (1.5 kg) **chicken parts**

1 lb (500 g) peeled **plum tomatoes** (see **PEELING TOMATOES** below)

1¼ cup (310 mL) **tomato juice**

1 large **red onion**, diced

1 large **red bell pepper**, diced

4 **garlic cloves**, pressed

2 cups (500 mL) chopped **fresh parsley**

1 tsp (5 mL) **salt**

¼ tsp (1 mL) freshly ground **black pepper**

1. Preheat the oven to 350°F (180°C).

2. Place the chicken parts in a 9- x 13-inch (3.5-L) casserole dish.

3. Combine the remaining ingredients in a bowl and pour them evenly over the chicken.

4. Cover the casserole dish with aluminum foil and bake until the chicken is cooked through and falling off the bone, about 75 to 90 minutes. Serve hot.

PEELING TOMATOES

To peel tomatoes, score the bottom with an "X" and place in boiling water for 30 to 60 seconds, until the skin begins to blister and fall away. Remove and plunge into a bowl of ice water. Peel off the skin and discard.

CHICKEN ALFREDO
Serves 4

Pasta was one of my favorite meals when I could eat wheat. That's why I'm always finding ways to develop pasta dishes that are legal for the Specific Carbohydrate Diet. Although this dish is made with yogurt instead of cream, the addition of honey mellows the tartness perfectly. The result is a rich, creamy, authentic-tasting Alfredo. If you are following the SCD and can tolerate lactose, feel free to use store-bought yogurt instead of homemade lactose-free yogurt—just make sure the yogurt you buy isn't low-fat or nonfat. —JL

1. Fry the chicken in oil in a large pan until fully cooked. Remove from the heat and set aside.

2. In another pan, gently melt the butter with salt and freshly ground pepper on low heat until the butter begins to brown. Remove from the heat and set aside.

3. Using a double boiler on medium heat, continuously whisk the yogurt and egg yolk together while the mixture cooks for 10 minutes—if you don't keep whisking, the egg yolks will cook in clumps rather than blend smoothly with the yogurt.

4. Add the Parmesan, honey, and melted butter and whisk together until thoroughly combined.

5. Pour the sauce into the frying pan with the chicken and toss. Place the pan on a burner, and heat the chicken and sauce on low until completely warmed through. Serve over **SPAGHETTI SQUASH** (page 43), shredded and steamed zucchini, or Enoki mushrooms.

oil for frying

1½ lb (750 g) **boneless, skinless chicken breast** sliced in strips for stir-frying

2 Tbsp (30 mL) **butter**

3 pinches of **salt**

2 pinches of freshly ground **black pepper**

1 cup (250 mL) **YOGURT** (page 27) made from whole milk or half-and-half (10%) cream

1 large **egg yolk**

1 cup (250 mL) grated **Parmesan cheese**

2 Tbsp (30 mL) plus 1 tsp (5 mL) **honey**

CABBAGE ROLLS
Makes 12 cabbage rolls

Typically filled with beef and rice, the substitution of cauliflower for rice is perfect in these cabbage rolls. Here, cauliflower is steamed and mashed before adding the beef and rolling the cabbage leaves. This recipe calls for ground beef, but ground chicken can be used to produce a dish that is milder in flavor.

1 large **onion**, chopped

2 **garlic cloves**, pressed

olive oil

¼ cup (60 mL) **Italian parsley**, chopped

1½ cups (375 mL) **OVEN-ROASTED TOMATO SAUCE** (page 41)

1 lb (500 g) **ground beef**

1 large **egg**

1½ cups (375 mL) **CAULIFLOWER MASH** (page 116, steps 1 to 5)

salt and freshly ground **black pepper**

1 large head of **green cabbage**

1. Cook the garlic and onions with a bit of oil in a medium-sized pan over medium heat. Sauté until fragrant and the onions are soft, about 5 minutes.

2. Stir in the Italian parsley and ½ cup (125 mL) of the tomato sauce. Heat through and remove from the stove.

3. Add the beef in a large bowl together with the egg, the onion mixture, and the mashed cauliflower. Mix well. Add generous amounts of salt and freshly ground pepper and refrigerate.

4. Remove the damaged outer leaves of the cabbage and set aside—do not discard.

5. Carefully remove the core from the base of the cabbage—this can be a challenge. Use a small, sharp paring knife and dig deep.

6. Bring a large pot of salted water to a boil and submerge the entire head of cabbage. Boil until the leaves are soft and pliable. Turn off the burner and with the cabbage still in the pot, use 2 forks to carefully remove the leaves from the head. Once removed, transfer them to a bowl of cold water to cool them and make them easier to handle. You will need 12 leaves or a combination of smaller torn leaves to make 12 rolls.

7. Preheat the oven to 350°F (180°C).

8. Lay the larger damaged outer cabbage leaves that you put aside in the bottom of a 9- x 13-inch (3.5-L) casserole dish. This will help insulate the rolls and prevent them from burning while in the oven.

9. Remove the beef mixture from the refrigerator and lay 1 cabbage leaf on a dish towel to absorb the water. Cut the thick vein from the bottom of the leaves to make them easier to roll.

10. Spoon a full ⅓ cup (75 mL) of filling onto the end of a cabbage leaf and roll, tucking the sides in as you go. If the leaf tears, don't worry. You can use extra, smaller leaves as patches to fix any holes and when everything is baked, it (miraculously) tends to stay together. Repeat until all the rolls are made.

11. Place each roll, seam side down in the casserole dish.

12. Pour the remaining 1 cup (250 mL) of tomato sauce over the rolls and bake until cooked through, about 1½ hours. If, after the first hour of baking, the top of the rolls are sufficiently brown, cover the rolls with any remaining cabbage leaves to prevent burning.

13. Remove from the oven and serve.

OSSO BUCO

Serves 4 to 6

Osso buco is an Italian dish of slowly braised veal shanks and is an outstanding main course, perfect for company. When I called my uncle, Bernie Zucker, and asked him to teach me his osso buco recipe so I could include it in this book, he didn't hesitate. Bernie is a wonderful and generous chef, and from the first time I tried osso buco at his house, it became one of my favorites. As with many adapted Specific Carbohydrate Diet recipes, a few of the ingredients have been changed from the original without (Bernie and I agree) sacrificing flavor. —JB

6 **veal shanks**

butcher's twine

kosher salt and freshly ground **black pepper**

2 Tbsp (30 mL) **olive oil**, plus more to brown the veal shanks

1 Tbsp (15 mL) **sunflower oil**

2 **leeks**, chopped

1 large **onion**, chopped

4 **carrots**, coarsely chopped

2 **celery stalks**, coarsely chopped

2 **tomatoes**, coarsely chopped

6 **garlic cloves**, coarsely chopped

1 small **jalapeno pepper**, seeded and sliced into 3 strips

5 stems of fresh **Italian parsley**, leaves removed from stems and coarsely chopped

5 sprigs of **fresh thyme**, leaves removed from stems

5 sprigs of **fresh rosemary**, leaves removed from stems

1. Preheat the oven to 350°F (180°C).

2. Tie butcher's twine (not too tightly) around each shank to keep it round and prevent it from falling open while cooking.

3. Season the veal shanks with kosher salt and freshly ground pepper, and set aside.

4. Heat 2 Tbsp (30 mL) olive oil and 1 Tbsp (15 mL) sunflower oil in a heavy-bottomed frying pan over high heat.

5. Add the leeks, onions, carrots, and celery and cook until the onions are translucent. Do not brown. Lightly salt and pepper the vegetables.

6. Add the chopped tomatoes, garlic, and jalapeno and continue to sauté until the garlic is fragrant and the flavors are combined. Pour the vegetable mixture into a large ovenproof casserole dish with a lid.

7. Return the frying pan to the stove. Over high heat, add a bit more olive oil. Add the veal shanks to the frying pan and sear each side. It will take about 4 minutes for the first side and 2 minutes for the second side.

8. Remove the shanks and place them on top of the vegetables in the large casserole dish.

9. Add all the fresh herbs to the frying pan and sauté on low for a minute with a bit more olive oil if necessary.

10. Remove from the heat and add the herbs to the shanks in the casserole dish.

11. Add the bay leaves to the casserole dish.

12. Return the frying pan to the stove and turn the heat to high. Deglaze the pan by pouring in the white wine and scraping up the browned bits that cling to the bottom. Let the wine reduce by about half.

13. Pour the reduced wine over the veal.

14. Pour the tomato sauce over the veal.

15. Add the chicken stock so that the liquid in the casserole dish comes halfway up the side of the shanks.

16. Cover the casserole dish with a tight-fitting lid. To reinforce a tight seal and ensure that no steam escapes during the long braising process, place aluminum foil over the casserole dish before you put on the lid.

17. Place the casserole dish in the oven and bake until the meat falls from the bone, about 2½ hours—test for doneness with a fork. If the meat needs a bit more cooking, return the casserole to the oven for about 30 more minutes.

18. Remove from the oven. Leave covered to retain heat until ready to serve.

19. Transfer the veal to a serving dish and taste the liquid and vegetables. Adjust the seasoning with salt and freshly ground pepper if necessary.

20. Serve the meat with the vegetables, or strain the vegetables and serve the meat with the strained liquid and no vegetables. Either way, remove the butcher's twine from around each piece of veal before plating.

3 bay **leaves**

1 cup (250 mL) **dry white wine**

1½ cups (375 mL) **OVEN-ROASTED TOMATO SAUCE** (page 41)

1 cup (250 mL) **CHICKEN STOCK** (page 44)

BRAISED LAMB SHANKS

Serves 4

I love lamb shanks. When done well, they are so tender and flavorful that you won't want to stop eating them. This lamb shank recipe is no exception. Don't be put off by the number of ingredients and steps—it's really rather easy. The marinade can even be made in advance and everything is either a standard in your kitchen or basics you usually buy at your grocer. Honestly, it's worth it! When the meat falls from the bone, you know your shanks are done to perfection. –JB

MARINADE

¼ cup (60 mL) grated **ginger**

4 **garlic cloves**, minced

¼ cup (60 mL) chopped **Italian parsley**

2 Tbsp to ¼ cup (30 to 60 mL) **tomato juice**

2 Tbsp (30 mL) **red wine vinegar**

½ tsp (2 mL) **cumin**

¼ tsp (1 mL) ground **cinnamon**

¼ tsp (1 mL) **salt**

¼ tsp (1 mL) freshly ground **black pepper**

Combine all the ingredients in your food processor or standing blender and purée until smooth. Set aside in a large bowl.

LAMB SHANKS

1. Preheat the oven to 350°F (180°C).

2. Heat a bit of oil in a large frying pan until smoking.

3. Add the lamb shanks and sear them until they are brown on all sides.

4. Remove them from the pan and place them in the marinade. Coat the shanks completely and set aside.

5. In the fat that is left in the pan, sauté the onions until translucent.

6. Add the tomatoes, carrots, whole garlic cloves, and water and bring to a boil. Remove from the stove.

7. Transfer the shanks with the marinade into a roasting pan.

8. Pour the tomato mixture over the shanks and cover the roasting pan with aluminum foil.

9. Bake for 60 minutes. Remove the foil and bake until the meat falls from the bone, about 30 to 45 more minutes.

10. Remove the shanks and taste the braising liquid. Adjust the seasoning with salt and freshly ground pepper if necessary and serve over the shanks.

olive oil for frying

six 6- to 8-oz (175- to 250-g) **lamb shanks**

1 large **sweet onion**, thinly sliced

6 **Italian tomatoes**, coarsely chopped

2 **carrots**, coarsely chopped

6 whole **garlic cloves**, peeled

4 cups (1 L) **water**

salt and freshly ground **black pepper**

ROSEMARY AND MINT RACK OF LAMB
Serves 2

These lamb chops are quick and easy to make. Chef Robyn Goorevitch suggests pairing them with **CARAMELIZED ONION AND CELERY ROOT MASH** (page 115) and **BAKED HUBBARD SQUASH WITH HONEY AND CINNAMON** (page 126) for a perfect meal for two. Double and triple as necessary for 4 people or more.

2 **Frenched racks of lamb** (see "FRENCHED" below)

4 sprigs **fresh rosemary**

4 sprigs **fresh thyme**

8 **mint leaves**

2 **garlic cloves**, minced

2 tsp (10 mL) **oil**

1. Preheat the oven to 350°F (180°C) and line a baking sheet with parchment paper.

2. Lay the racks of lamb on the prepared baking sheet.

3. While the lamb comes to room temperature (allow 20 minutes only), strip the fresh herbs off their stems.

4. Place the rosemary, thyme, and mint in a coffee grinder and grind until chopped and totally combined, about 10 seconds.

5. Place the herbs in a bowl and add the minced garlic and oil. Mix well and spread evenly on top of the racks of lamb.

6. Bake until the lamb is medium rare and still pink inside, about 25 to 30 minutes.

"FRENCHED"

The term "Frenched" refers to the technique of removing the meat and other tissue from the ends of the lamb chop bones. Ask your butcher to do this for you.

STUFFED BURGERS

Serves 4

I don't have a barbecue or indoor grill and because I don't like to fry meat, I decided to pop my burgers in the oven and bake them on a grill rack (a metal rack with legs), which allows the fat to drip away. The burgers were tender and juicy, a lot like meatloaf (in a good way!). Feel free to change the ingredients used for stuffing—try tomato, onion, parsley, mushroom, or other kinds of cheese, such as blue or cheddar. You can also grill these burgers on a barbecue or fry them. —JL

1. Preheat the oven to 350°F (180°C).

2. Mix the beef, almond flour, tomato paste, freshly ground pepper, basil, salt, and eggs in a bowl until thoroughly combined.

3. Form 8 small burger patties.

4. Sandwich 1 chunk of cheese, 1 zucchini slice, and 1 slice of garlic between 2 burger patties. Press the edges together to seal. Repeat until all the burgers are formed.

5. Place a grill rack in a 9- x 13-inch (3.5-L) casserole dish and place the burgers on the rack.

6. Bake until cooked through, about 30 minutes.

1 lb (500 g) lean **ground beef**

½ cup (125 mL) **almond flour**

1 Tbsp (15 mL) **TOMATO PASTE** (page 42)

¼ tsp (1 mL) freshly ground **black pepper**

½ tsp (2 mL) **dried basil**

½ tsp (2 mL) **salt**

2 large **eggs**

4 chunks of **Parmesan cheese**

4 **zucchini** slices

1 to 2 **garlic cloves**, cut into 4 thin slices

"SPAGHETTI" AND MEATBALLS

Serves 6 to 8

I used to love eating spaghetti and meatballs so much that when dining out, I would always pick this comfort food despite the endless possibilities on the menu. These meatballs can be enjoyed alone or served over your favorite pasta substitute, such as **SPAGHETTI SQUASH** (page 43), shredded and steamed zucchini or Enoki mushrooms. You can also try them over **BASIC BISCUITS** (page 56) or **CHEDDAR CHEESE BISCUITS** (page 57). If you don't follow the Specific Carbohydrate Diet or your symptoms are in remission, feel free to use one 28-oz (796-mL) can of plum tomatoes with juice instead of the peeled plum tomatoes and tomato juice. —JL

1 lb (500 g) **ground beef**

1 large **egg**

2 **garlic cloves**, minced

¼ cup (60 mL) grated **Parmesan cheese**

¼ tsp (1 mL) **salt**

¼ tsp (1 mL) ground **cinnamon**

¼ cup (60 mL) minced **fresh parsley**

½ cup (125 mL) **almond flour**

2 Tbsp (30 mL) **olive oil**

1 **small onion**, minced

1 lb (500 g) peeled **plum tomatoes** (see **PEELING TOMATOES** on page 152)

1¼ cups (310 mL) **tomato juice**

1. Thoroughly combine the beef, egg, garlic, cheese, salt, cinnamon, parsley, and almond flour in a bowl.

2. Form into small balls about the size of a walnut.

3. Heat the oil in a frying pan over medium heat. Add the meatballs—don't crowd them. Cook them in more than 1 batch if necessary. Turn the meatballs every few minutes as they cook.

4. When the meatballs are browned all over (after about 15 minutes), transfer them to a plate and turn off the heat.

5. Pour some, but not all, of the fat out of the pan and turn the heat back to medium. Cook the onion in the frying pan and stir until it begins to brown.

6. Crush the tomatoes with a fork or your hands and add them with the tomato juice to the pan. Cook for 5 to 10 minutes.

7. Add the meatballs to the sauce and cook for about 15 more minutes.

8. Serve over your choice of pasta substitute or biscuits.

SHEPHERD'S PIE
Serves 6 to 8

This recipe provides a new twist on shepherd's pie. Squash is used instead of the traditional potato topping and you can substitute chicken or turkey for the beef.

TOPPING

1. Preheat the oven to 375°F (190°C).

2. Cut the squash in half. Do not remove the seeds.

3. Pour enough water to cover the bottom of a 9- x 13-inch (3.5-L) casserole dish and place the squash pieces cut side down in the dish.

4. Bake until the squash is a bit soft when you press down on it, about 30 to 40 minutes.

5. Remove the squash from the oven and reduce the heat to 350°F (180°C).

6. Remove the seeds from the cooked squash and discard. Scoop the flesh from the squash and mash until smooth.

7. Add the butter, salt, and freshly ground pepper, and mix well.

8. Let the mixture cool in the refrigerator and store there until ready for final assembly.

3 lb (1.5 kg) **butternut squash**

1 Tbsp (15 mL) **butter**

¼ tsp (1 mL) **salt**

1 pinch of freshly ground **black pepper**

continued on next page

FILLING

1 **onion,** chopped

3 **garlic cloves**, finely chopped

2 large **carrots**, peeled and chopped

2 lb (1 kg) **ground beef**

⅔ cup (150 mL) **TOMATO PASTE** (page 42)

2 tsp (10 mL) **red wine vinegar**

¼ tsp (1 mL) freshly ground **black pepper**

½ tsp (2 mL) **dried thyme**

½ tsp (2 mL) **dried oregano**

1 tsp (5 mL) **salt**

1. Sauté the onion, garlic, and carrot in a medium-sized pot over medium heat for 5 minutes.

2. Add the beef, tomato paste, red wine vinegar, and spices, and cook until the meat is browned.

ASSEMBLY AND BAKING

1 large **egg**, beaten

paprika and grated **Parmesan cheese** for sprinkling

1. Preheat the oven to 350°F (180°C).

2. Remove the squash mixture from the refrigerator and thoroughly mix in the egg.

3. Evenly spread the browned beef in a 9- x 13-inch (3.5-L) casserole dish and evenly spread the squash mixture over top.

4. Sprinkle the squash liberally with paprika and Parmesan cheese.

5. Bake until cooked through, about 30 minutes.

DRY-RUB STEAK SPICE

Makes about ¼ cup (60 mL)

This dry rub is full of flavor and it's all you will need to season your steak or roast. As always, use the best cut of meat for the best results. Our favorite is beef tenderloin. For another dry-rub blend, see **DRY-RUB SALMON BARBECUED ON A CEDAR PLANK** (page 142).

1. Combine all the ingredients in a coffee grinder and pulse a few times. Stop before the spices become too finely ground—they should still have some texture.

2. Rub the steak spice over your choice cut of meat and let it sit for 15 minutes before barbecuing or oven-roasting as usual.

3. Store leftover spice in the freezer, where it will keep indefinitely.

2 Tbsp (30 mL) **salt**

2 Tbsp (30 mL) **whole yellow mustard seed**

2 Tbsp (30 mL) **dried garlic flakes**

1 Tbsp (15 mL) plus 1 tsp (5 mL) coarsely ground **black pepper**

1 Tbsp (15 mL) plus 1 tsp (5 mL) **coriander seeds**

1 tsp (5 mL) **red pepper flakes**

IT'S A CHICKEN THING

If you grind the Dry-Rub Steak Spice to a fine powder, it's great on chicken wings, legs, and thighs. When the spice-coated chicken pieces are baked in the oven or grilled on the barbecue, they form a crisp, spicy crust that locks in the moisture.

DESSERTS

Who doesn't love dessert? Even if you only eat a small bite, your favorite sweet treat can be the perfect end to a meal. In this section, we've got everything your sweet tooth might desire: ice cream, candy, cookies, pie, cakes, and fancy fruit. For more dessert ideas, see **DESSERT FOR BREAKFAST AND BREAKING OTHER MEALTIME BARRIERS** (page 207).

WARMED CRÊPES WITH JAM À LA MODE

Serves 4

I used to love warmed crêpes as a kid. My mother would make them, but I swear she served them for dinner rather than dessert! Serve with any of the **HONEY SYRUPS** (pages 37 to 38), or with **CARAMEL SAUCE** (page 177) and **CLASSIC VANILLA ICE CREAM** (page 191) as suggested in this recipe. —JB

12 to 16 **BASIC CRÊPES** (page 48)

1 cup (250 mL) **RASPBERRY JAM**
(page 40)

CLASSIC VANILLA ICE CREAM
(page 191) and **CARAMEL SAUCE**
(page 177) to taste

1. Preheat the oven to 300°F (150°C) and butter a 9- x 13-inch (3.5-L) casserole dish.

2. Carefully spread the jam on each crêpe and roll into a cigar shape.

3. Place the crêpes side by side in a single layer in the prepared dish.

4. Bake until warmed through and crispy around the edges, about 5 minutes.

5. Divide the crêpes among 4 plates and top with a scoop of vanilla ice cream and a drizzle of caramel sauce.

GRILLED PEACHES WITH SWEETENED YOGURT CHEESE

Serves 4

The freshness of in-season ripe peaches grilled on the barbecue—it is the essence of summer. For this dessert, it's best to use freestone peaches. However, if none are available, quickly slice each peach in half with a sharp, heavy cleaver, cutting through the entire pit. Use a sharp filleting knife to then remove the pit from both halves of the peach.

1. Preheat the oven or toaster oven to 300°F (150°C).

2. Toast the almonds in the oven for 5 to 10 minutes, until lightly browned. Remove from the oven and let cool.

3. Preheat the barbecue to medium heat.

4. Combine the yogurt cheese, honey, and vanilla.

5. Cover and cool in the refrigerator.

6. Cut each peach in half and remove the pit.

7. Brush the peach halves with a bit of melted butter and place them cut side down on the barbecue.

8. Close the barbecue lid and grill for 3 to 4 minutes, until the peaches are tender and lightly colored.

9. Remove and place on a serving platter.

10. Fold ¼ cup (60 mL) of the toasted, sliced almonds into the yogurt cheese immediately before serving.

11. Evenly divide the cheese among the 4 peach halves and sprinkle with the rest of the sliced almonds.

12. Serve warm.

½ cup (125 mL) **YOGURT CHEESE** (page 28)

1 Tbsp (15 mL) **honey**

1 tsp (5 mL) **PURE VANILLA EXTRACT** (page 36)

2 ripe **peaches**

melted **butter** for brushing on peaches

⅓ cup (75 mL) sliced **almonds**

RUSTIC PEARS

Serves 4

My friend Tracy Barber is the founder of Inner Hero Pilates, a company dedicated to Pilates training and nutritional counseling. One of her many talents is improvising quick, simple, healthy meals. One year for my birthday, she made me dinner and developed this dessert. –JL

1 Tbsp (15 mL) **unsalted butter**

2 soft, ripe **pears**

1 cup (250 mL) **fresh wild blueberries** or **frozen blueberries**

½ cup (125 mL) **walnut pieces**

2 Tbsp (30 mL) **honey**

1. Preheat the oven to 350°F (180°C) and grease a small casserole dish with butter.

2. Wash the pears and slice them in half lengthwise. Remove their cores and stems, but don't peel them.

3. Rub the butter on the pear skins.

4. Place the pears in the casserole dish skin side down.

5. Combine the blueberries and walnut pieces in a small bowl.

6. Spoon the blueberry-walnut mixture over the pears, filling up the holes where the cores and stems used to be. Don't worry if the mixture topples off the pears—that's the rustic part!

7. Drizzle the honey over the pears.

8. Place in the oven on the center rack and bake until soft, about 20 minutes.

9. Let cool for 5 minutes before serving.

10. Store the leftovers in the refrigerator and reheat or eat them cold for a quick, healthy breakfast.

STRAWBERRY-RHUBARB MINI GALETTES

Makes 6 tarts

Our readers and cooking-class students let us know that the Apple Galette was one of their favorite recipes from our first cookbook, *Grain-Free Gourmet: Delicious Recipes for Healthy Living*. This free-form, rustic method of pie making is quick and easy. So here we give you another galette recipe, in this case, individual mini galettes made with strawberry and rhubarb. Although the instructions here are for individual pies, you may choose to make one large pie—simply follow the same instructions but roll out one large crust instead of 6 small ones. Serve as is, drizzled with **CARAMEL SAUCE** (page 177), or with a side of **CLASSIC VANILLA ICE CREAM** (page 191).

CRUST

1. Mix all the crust ingredients in a bowl using a fork and then your hands, until the dough comes together in a ball. Flatten the ball and make a thick, even disk. Wrap it in plastic wrap and refrigerate.

2. Cut 6 pieces of parchment paper into squares of about 6½ x 6½ inches (17 x 17 cm).

3. Once cold, divide the dough into 6 equal pieces and place each one on parchment paper.

4. Roll the pieces of dough into balls and flatten them into disks using the palms of your hands.

5. Cover a disk with a piece of plastic wrap and, using a rolling pin, gently roll out the disk to about 6 inches (15 cm) in diameter.

6. Remove the plastic wrap and use it for the next disk, repeating the process until all the dough is rolled out.

7. Transfer each dough round, still on its piece of parchment paper, onto a baking sheet and place it in the refrigerator until you are ready to assemble the galettes.

2 cups (500 mL) **almond flour**

¼ cup (60 mL) **unsalted butter**, at room temperature

3 Tbsp (45 mL) **honey**

¼ tsp (1 mL) **baking soda**

½ tsp (2 mL) **salt**

continued on next page

FILLING

1 lb (500 g) **frozen rhubarb**, thawed

⅓ cup (75 mL) **honey**

1 tsp (5 mL) freshly squeezed **lemon juice**

1 tsp (5 mL) grated **orange rind**

2 cups (500 mL) sliced **strawberries**

1. Drain any accumulated water from the thawed rhubarb.

2. Cook the rhubarb and the honey in a medium-sized pot over medium heat until the rhubarb is soft but not entirely a purée, about 7 to 10 minutes.

3. Add the lemon juice and the orange rind and stir.

4. Let the entire mixture cool and thicken in the refrigerator.

5. When cool, stir in the strawberries.

ASSEMBLY AND BAKING

1. Preheat the oven to 325°F (160°C).

2. Remove the dough rounds from the refrigerator.

3. Lift 1 chilled crust, still on the parchment paper, from the baking sheet and place it on the countertop in front of you.

4. Scoop ½ cup (125 mL) of the filling and place it in the center of the round.

5. Use the parchment paper to help fold the dough up and around the filling, turning the parchment paper as you go. Pinch together any tears in the dough. Return the mini galette, still on the parchment paper, to the baking sheet and repeat the process with the remaining rounds.

6. Bake the galettes until the crust is golden brown, about 20 to 25 minutes.

7. Serve warm.

APPLE CAKE
Serves 8 to 12

This cake rises high and is light and airy. Enjoy it on its own or drizzled with **CARAMEL SAUCE** (page 177) and sprinkled with chopped **CANDIED PECANS** (page 45).

1. Preheat the oven to 325°F (160°C) and grease a 10-inch (3-L) springform pan.

2. Peel and slice each apple into 16 slices.

3. Combine the almond flour, cinnamon, salt, and baking soda in a large bowl.

4. In a smaller bowl, lightly beat the eggs; then mix in the honey and vanilla.

5. Stir in the lemon juice.

6. Add the dry ingredients to the wet and mix thoroughly. **At this point, you will notice that the batter is rising and bubbly. You should try to move through the next steps quickly to take advantage of this chemical reaction, which will help to create a really high and light cake**.

7. Add the sliced apples, mix thoroughly, and pour into the prepared springform pan.

8. Bake for 30 minutes.

9. After 30 minutes, cover with aluminum foil and bake until the cake is firm on the sides but softer in the middle, about 45 more minutes.

10. Remove from the oven and let the cake cool before releasing it from the springform pan.

2 lb (1 kg) (about 5 medium-sized) **apples**, any combination of Mitsu, Fuji, or Golden Delicious

2 cups (500 mL) **almond flour**

1 Tbsp (15 mL) ground **cinnamon**

½ tsp (2 mL) **salt**

2 tsp (10 mL) **baking soda**

4 large **eggs**

¾ cup (175 mL) **honey**

2 tsp (10 mL) **PURE VANILLA EXTRACT** (page 36)

¼ cup (60 mL) freshly squeezed **lemon juice**

LEMON FREEZE
Serves 8

"WOW!" is exactly what I exclaimed when I first tasted this dessert. I was floored by how light and delicious it is. And it's so easy! Only the crust is baked in the oven and, when filled, it is simply frozen—it's the perfect make-ahead dessert. If you're not lactose-intolerant, you can use store-bought yogurt in the filling instead of homemade lactose-free yogurt—just make sure the yogurt you buy isn't low-fat or non-fat. —JB

CRUST

1. Preheat the oven to 325°F (160°C).

2. Mix all the crust ingredients in a bowl using a fork and then your hands, until the dough comes together in a ball.

3. Flatten the dough into a disk.

4. Lift the removable base from a 10-inch (25-cm) flan pan and cover it with a piece of parchment paper cut to fit. Place the flattened dough onto the parchment paper.

5. Cover with a piece of plastic wrap and roll the dough out to the edges of the parchment paper.

6. Return the base with the rolled-out dough to the flan ring and, with your fingers, gently press the edges of the dough about a ¼ inch (5 mm) or so up the sides of the pan.

7. Bake until lightly browned, about 5 to 7 minutes.

8. Let cool.

1½ cups (375 mL) **almond flour**

3 Tbsp (45 mL) **unsalted butter**, at room temperature

2 Tbsp (30 mL) **honey**

1 pinch of **baking soda**

¼ tsp (1 mL) **salt**

continued on next page

FILLING AND ASSEMBLY

3 large **egg yolks**

¼ cup (60 mL) **honey**

¼ cup (60 mL) freshly squeezed **lemon juice**

grated **rind of ½ lemon**

3 **egg whites**, beaten stiff

½ cup (125 mL) **YOGURT** (page 27) made from whole milk or half-and-half (10%) cream

1. Whisk together the egg yolks, honey, lemon juice, and lemon rind in a double boiler or in a glass bowl sitting above a pot of boiling water. Cook the mixture until it turns from thin, frothy, and bright yellow to thick, creamy, and butter-colored, about 10 to 15 minutes.

2. Remove from the heat and let cool at room temperature. You can speed up this process by placing the glass bowl in a larger bowl filled with ice and water, stirring the lemon mixture occasionally.

3. Beat the egg whites until stiff.

4. Gently fold the yogurt into the cooled lemon mixture.

5. Gently fold in the beaten egg whites.

6. Pour the entire mixture into the cooled crust and freeze.

7. Remove from the freezer and let stand in the refrigerator for 20 minutes before serving.

REDUCING LACTOSE

If you are sensitive to lactose, you can use organic cream in small amounts if you add liquid lactase, available at drugstores as Lactaid or Lacteeze drops. Be sure to follow the instructions on the package carefully.

CARAMEL FONDUE

Makes 2 cups (500 mL), enough to serve 4 to 6

When I was a child growing up in Montreal, we used to spend our winter weekends skiing in Stowe, Vermont. One of our favorite restaurants in Stowe was the Swiss Pot, where they served fondue—both cheese and chocolate. This dessert is inspired by the chocolate fondue I craved as a kid and still love as an adult. The suggestions for dipping foods and toppings are just that—suggestions. Feel free to invent your own combinations. This fondue is best served in a ceramic bowl over a warming candle, the kind you would typically use for chocolate fondue. Make sure you have enough long fondue forks for everyone. Savor this dessert slowly and leisurely. It's perfect for meals during which the conversation is so good, you never really want to leave the table. —JB

CARAMEL SAUCE

1. Bring the honey to a boil in a medium-sized pot over high heat.

2. Boil for 2 to 3 minutes. Lower the heat to medium.

3. Add the butter and stir until melted.

4. Carefully add the cream. The mixture will bubble up. Continue to stir until the sauce is slightly thickened and coats the back of a spoon, about 2 to 3 minutes.

5. To store the caramel sauce for later use, transfer it to a glass jar and keep it in the refrigerator. It will thicken as it cools.

1 cup (250 mL) **honey**

½ cup (125 mL) **butter**

½ cup (125 mL) lactose-treated **organic half-and-half** (10%) cream (see **REDUCING LACTOSE** on page 176)

DIPPING FOODS

- coarsely chopped **bananas, apples**, and **pears**
- whole **grapes**
- **clementine orange** segments

REHEATING AND ASSEMBLY

1. Gently reheat the thickened caramel sauce on the stove or in the microwave until it is fluid and warm, and transfer it to a small ceramic bowl or fondue pot set above a tea-light candle.

2. Serve the chopped fruit and toppings each in a separate bowl.

3. Dip the fruit into the warm caramel sauce and then into the topping of your choice.

TOPPINGS

- chopped **pecans**, chopped **roasted almond**, chopped **cashews**, chopped **hazelnuts**
- desiccated **unsweetened coconut**
- **sunflower seeds**
- **sesame seeds**
- **raisins**

CAPPUCCINO DACQUOISE
Makes one 9-inch (23-cm) cake

After a year of asking my friend (and exceptional baker and chef) Randy Rosen if she could show me how to make her butter cream for a cappuccino dacquoise, I finally made a date to see her. Randy rifled through her cookbooks and found the recipe for a classic butter cream using honey rather than sugar to accommodate my diet—she then transformed this simple butter cream into a cappuccino dream. A note about meringues—it's hard to get a dry, crisp meringue when you use honey instead of sugar. For this reason, the meringue is baked and dried in the oven overnight. Don't try to rush this part—it really does take time. Frost this cake hours before serving if you want the meringue to be soft or frost it minutes before serving if you want to maintain the crunch of the meringue between the layers of cream—either way, it's delicious! –JB

MERINGUE LAYERS

9 large **egg whites**

1 tsp (5 mL) **PURE VANILLA EXTRACT** (page 36)

½ cup (125 mL) **honey**, warmed

1½ cups (375 mL) **almond flour**

1. Preheat the oven to 175°F (85°C).

2. Draw three 9-inch (23-cm) circles on parchment paper and place the paper circle-side down on 2 baking sheets.

3. With an electric mixer on high, beat the egg whites until they are frothy.

4. Add the vanilla.

5. While the mixer is running, drizzle in the warm honey and continue beating until the egg whites are very stiff.

6. Fold the almond flour into the stiff whites by hand.

7. Using a spoon or a pastry bag, fill in the three circles with even amounts of the egg mixture.

8. Bake for 3 hours. Turn the oven down to 170°F (80°C) (or as close to that as you are able to set your oven control), and leave the meringue layers in the oven until they feel fairly dry and crisp, between 12 and 24 hours. The meringues will shrink considerably in height and take on a golden brown color because of the honey.

9. Remove the meringues from the oven. Allow them to cool and gently remove them from the parchment paper.

CAPPUCCINO BUTTER CREAM

1. Beat the egg yolks on high until pale and thick, about 6 minutes.

2. Heat the honey to a rolling boil.

3. Immediately pour the honey into a glass measuring cup to stop the cooking process.

4. Pour a little bit of the honey on top of the egg yolks and beat on high for 5 seconds. Repeat until all the honey has been used. Continue to beat on high until the mixture is cold (touching the bottom of the mixing bowl will tell you if the mixture is warm or cold).

5. Slowly and patiently add the butter a small pat at a time while mixing on high. Continue until all the butter has been used. The mixture should be completely incorporated, light, and smooth.

6. Add the cooled coffee, mixing slowly at first and then at high speed to incorporate.

6 large **egg yolks**

⅓ cup (75 mL) **honey**

2 lb (1 kg) **unsalted butter**, at room temperature—make sure your butter has no added water

2 Tbsp (30 mL) **strong coffee**, made from ¼ cup (60 mL) boiling water and 3 Tbsp (45 mL) espresso coffee, cooled to room temperature and filtered to remove the grounds

⅓ cup (75 mL) chopped, **roasted almonds** or **hazelnuts** for decorating

ASSEMBLY

1. Spread a thin layer of the butter cream on the first meringue and stack with the next. Repeat until all the layers are stacked.

2. Finish with a layer of butter cream. Frost the sides and, if you are feeling creative, decorate the top of the cake with florets of butter cream using a pastry bag with a flower tip.

3. Sprinkle with the chopped nuts.

GLAZED POUND CAKE

Makes one 9- x 5-inch (2-L) loaf

I'm always looking for ways to make food preparation faster and easier. During one of my attempted shortcuts, I poured the batter for **WAFFLES AND PANCAKES** (page 61) into a pan and baked it, hoping that it would be edible. The loaf's texture was a bit chewy, but the taste was unmistakable—vanilla cake. This invention may not sound terribly exciting, but when you have been unable to enjoy a nice plain cake for years due to allergies or illness, its rediscovery is truly a cause for celebration. Several batches later, I perfected the recipe and added a light glaze. Now you can serve guests a moist, sweet cake that can be topped with fruit, any ice cream (pages 189 to 194), or, better yet, birthday candles. —JL

CAKE

2 cups (500 mL) finely ground **almond flour** (see **FINELY GROUND ALMOND FLOUR** on page 54)

½ tsp (2 mL) **baking soda**

½ tsp (2 mL) **salt**

¼ cup (60 mL) **honey**

1 Tbsp (15 mL) **PURE VANILLA EXTRACT** (page 36)

3 large **eggs**

1. Preheat the oven to 300°F (150°C) and line a greased 9 x 5 inch (2-L) loaf pan with parchment paper.

2. Mix the almond flour, baking soda, and salt in a bowl.

3. Add the honey, vanilla, and eggs to the flour mixture and whisk together until combined thoroughly and smooth.

4. Pour the batter into the prepared loaf pan and bake until a knife comes out clean when inserted, about 40 minutes.

5. Let cool.

GLAZE

3 Tbsp (45 mL) **honey**

2 Tbsp (30 mL) **butter**, melted

¼ tsp (1 mL) **PURE VANILLA EXTRACT** (page 36)

1. Mix all ingredients together in a bowl until the glaze is even in color and texture. It should be runny and a little warm from the melted butter.

2. Let cool to room temperature.

ASSEMBLY

1. Place the cooled loaf on a serving plate. Drizzle the glaze over top, allowing it to run down the sides of the loaf.

2. Refrigerate until the glaze is set, at least 1 hour.

TIRAMISU

Serves 6 to 8

Some of my best ideas come from watching others eat something I can't. This recipe was inspired by a generous helping of tiramisu served at a family celebration and shared by everyone—except me. I immediately set to work creating lactose-free, grain-free tiramisu. It only took me a couple of tries to get this basic tiramisu recipe just right. It provides the perfect end to an Italian meal such as **"SPAGHETTI" AND MEATBALLS** (page 162) or **CHICKEN ALFREDO** (page 153). If you don't follow the Specific Carbohydrate Diet and aren't lactose-intolerant, feel free to use mascarpone cheese instead of **YOGURT CHEESE** (page 28) made from whipping cream yogurt. —JL

COFFEE SYRUP

1. Pour the honey into the espresso and mix well.

2. Set aside to cool.

¾ cup (175 mL) **hot espresso** made from 1 cup (250 mL) boiling water and 2 Tbsp (30 mL) espresso coffee, filtered to remove the grounds (see **HELPFUL HINTS** on page 183)

3 Tbsp (45 mL) **honey**

CAKES

1. Preheat the oven to 310°F (155°C) and line a baking sheet with parchment paper.

2. Combine the almond flour and baking soda in a bowl.

3. In another bowl, combine the butter, honey, yogurt, and egg and mix well.

4. Add the dry ingredients to the wet and mix well.

5. Separate the dough into 6 equal balls and form into 3-inch (8-cm) rounds that are ¾-inch (2-cm) thick.

6. Place the rounds 2 inches (5 cm) apart on the prepared baking sheet and bake until golden brown, about 15 to 18 minutes.

7. Remove from the oven and cool.

2 cups (500 mL) **almond flour**

½ tsp (2 mL) **baking soda**

¼ cup (60 mL) **butter**, melted

1 Tbsp (15 mL) **honey**

¼ cup (60 mL) **YOGURT** (page 27)

1 large **egg**

continued on next page

CREAM FILLING

1. Combine the egg yolks, honey, and vanilla using a double boiler and whisk until the mixture bubbles or is heated through. Let it cook for about 5 minutes, whisking constantly.

2. Mix in ¼ cup (60 mL) of the coffee syrup and let the custard cool.

3. When cool, add the yogurt cheese and mix well. The refrigerated cheese will be very stiff, so try breaking it up with a fork when you first start incorporating it into the custard. When the cheese is in smaller chunks, use a whisk to blend the mixture until it is smooth.

3 large **egg yolks**

¼ to ⅓ cup (60 to 75 mL) **honey**

1 Tbsp (15 mL) **PURE VANILLA EXTRACT** (page 36)

¼ cup (60 mL) of the **COFFEE SYRUP**

3 cups (750 mL) refrigerated **YOGURT CHEESE** made from **YOGURT** (page 27) made with whipping cream (unrefrigerated yogurt cheese will be too runny) (see **HELPFUL HINTS** below)

ASSEMBLY

1. Cut the cakes in half vertically so they are shaped like half moons. You may also slice them in half horizontally to create thinner cake layers.

2. Arrange 1 layer of cake in an 8-inch (2-L) square casserole dish.

3. Spoon about one-third of the remaining coffee syrup over the cakes.

4. Spread one-third of the cream filling over the cakes.

5. Repeat steps 2 to 4 until you have 3 layers of each, finishing with a cream layer.

6. Sprinkle with cinnamon and allow it to set in the refrigerator for at least 3 hours.

ground **cinnamon** for sprinkling

HELPFUL HINTS

- If you don't have any espresso on hand, use strong, dark roast coffee instead.

- You will need to drip 4 cups (1 L) of whipping cream **YOGURT** (page 27) to make about 3 cups (750 mL) of **YOGURT CHEESE** (page 28).

PEANUT BUTTER ICE BOX TRUFFLES

Makes 24 truffles

We're not quite sure why these truffles taste great at room temperature, but even better when frozen. They are the perfect not-too-sweet something to make one day and store in the freezer to eat when a craving hits. Whether you bring them out to share with company or keep them for yourself, these truffles are a wholesome yet indulgent treat.

1 cup (250 mL) unsweetened, unsalted **peanut butter**

¼ cup (60 mL) **honey**

1 pinch of **salt**

1 cup (250 mL) finely chopped **dates**

1 cup (250 mL) chopped **pecans**

unsweetened **desiccated coconut**

hazelnut meal

1. Heat the peanut butter and honey over low heat until entirely melted.

2. Remove from the heat and stir in the salt, dates, and pecans.

3. Allow the mixture to cool completely.

4. Place the coconut and hazelnut meal in separate shallow bowls.

5. When cool, form the peanut butter mixture into small balls and roll each one in either the coconut or the hazelnut meal.

6. Store in the freezer and serve frozen.

PEANUT BUTTER CARAMEL CRISPS
Makes 20 to 24 candies

Jodi and I have taught many cooking classes, and this recipe is one of our students' favorites. Its original name was Easter Candy and was demonstrated during the 2006 holiday class. It probably became so popular because it is reminiscent of a peanut-buttery candy bar from your past and is guaranteed to provide every sweet tooth with instant gratification. —JL

FILLING

1. Line a baking sheet with parchment paper.

2. Thoroughly mix all of the filling ingredients in a bowl.

3. Spread the peanut butter mixture ¼ inch (5 mm) thick onto the prepared baking sheet.

½ cup (125 mL) unsweetened, unsalted **peanut butter**

2 Tbsp (30 mL) **butter**, melted

¼ cup (60 mL) **honey**

TOFFEE COATING

1. Boil the honey in a medium-sized pot on low to medium-low heat until it reaches 300°F (150°C) on a candy thermometer, about 6 to 8 minutes. The honey should boil as vigorously as it can without boiling over. Stir the honey as it boils.

2. Turn the heat off when the honey has finished cooking, but keep the pot on the hot burner.

3. Add the butter and nut butter to the honey. Mix thoroughly.

1 cup (250 mL) **honey**

2 Tbsp (30 mL) **butter**

1 cup (250 mL) **cashew, almond,** or **hazelnut butter**

ASSEMBLY

1. Working quickly, pour the toffee over the peanut butter filling until it is completely covered. If the toffee becomes too stiff, reheat it until it is fluid enough to work with.

2. When the candy starts to set, but is still soft enough to cut, slice it into small squares using a pizza cutter or long, sharp knife.

3. Put the candies in the refrigerator until they harden.

4. Remove hardened candies to an airtight container, separating each layer with parchment paper. Store in the refrigerator for 1 to 2 weeks or in the freezer for 2 to 3 months.

GINGER COOKIES

Makes 18 to 20 cookies

Taste can be a powerful memory trigger. When I eat these cookies, I immediately think of winter. Their spices remind me of holiday cheer, brightly lit fireplaces, and gentle snowfalls. —JL

2½ cups (625 mL) **almond flour**

2 tsp (10 mL) ground **cinnamon**

1½ tsp (7 mL) ground **ginger**

½ tsp (2 mL) ground **cloves**

¼ tsp (1 mL) **salt**

½ cup (125 mL) **butter**, softened or partially melted

⅓ cup (75 mL) **honey**

1 large **egg**

1 tsp (5 mL) **PURE VANILLA EXTRACT** (page 36)

1. Preheat the oven to 325°F (160°C) and line a baking sheet with parchment paper.

2. Combine the almond flour, cinnamon, ginger, cloves, and salt in a large bowl.

3. In another bowl, add the butter, honey, egg, and vanilla and combine well.

4. Add the dry ingredients to the wet and mix thoroughly.

5. Flatten 2-Tbsp (30-mL) balls of dough between the palms of your hands until each cookie is ¼ inch (5 mm) thick. Place on the prepared baking sheet.

6. Bake until starting to brown, about 12 to 15 minutes. Let cool before serving.

SHAPED HOLIDAY COOKIES

You can make shaped holiday cookies with this dough using a cookie cutter. Simply place the cookie cutter on a baking sheet lined with parchment paper and spoon some of the dough into the cookie cutter. Press the dough down with your fingers until it is spread evenly and about ¼ inch (5 mm) thick. Lift the cookie cutter and repeat until the baking sheet is filled.

CASHEW BUTTER COOKIES
Makes 18 to 20 cookies

Sometimes a small change can make a big difference. This recipe is essentially a peanut butter cookie recipe made with cashew butter instead. If you close your eyes while you chew, these cashew treats taste remarkably similar to plain chocolate cookies!

1. Preheat the oven to 325°F (160°C) and line a baking sheet with parchment paper.

2. Mix the almond flour and baking soda in a bowl.

3. In another bowl, mix the cashew butter, eggs, butter, vanilla, and honey.

4. Add the dry ingredients to the wet and mix well.

5. Drop the batter in 2-Tbsp (30-mL) mounds onto the prepared baking sheet.

6. Bake for about 10 minutes—be careful not to overcook. These are best when eaten moist or "ooey gooey." If they start to brown, they have cooked too long. While baking, the cookies should rise and spread, but remain light in color.

7. Let cool before serving and store in the refrigerator or freezer with sheets of parchment paper between the cookie layers so they don't stick together. To enjoy them warm again, simply pop them in the microwave and reheat for a few seconds.

1 cup (250 mL) **almond flour**

¼ tsp (1 mL) **baking soda**

1 cup (250 mL) **cashew butter**

2 large **eggs**

2 Tbsp (30 mL) **butter**, melted

1 tsp (5 mL) **PURE VANILLA EXTRACT** (page 36)

½ cup (125 mL) **honey**

HONEY-FREE OPTION

I once made these cookies without honey. It was an accident, of course. I remember my frustration as I tried to mix the unusually stiff batter and realized after I had put the cookies in the oven, that I had forgotten a key ingredient. But to my surprise and delight, the end product was delicious. The cookies had the texture of shortbread and the natural sweetness of the cashews compensated for the lack of honey. So for a totally different cashew cookie experience, simply omit the honey. –JL

CASHEW BUTTER BROWNIES
Makes 25 pieces

This recipe is a variation of a peanut butter brownie recipe that has been floating around the Specific Carbohydrate Diet community for a number of years. Its provenance is unknown, but it has become a favorite of many. Here we use cashew butter instead of unsweetened peanut butter with fantastically rich, creamy, and wonderful results. Remember, the only ingredient here that has to cook is the egg, so don't overbake these brownies or they will become crumbly and lose the moistness that is their trademark.

2 cups (500 mL) **cashew butter**

2 large **eggs**

½ cup (125 mL) **honey**

½ tsp (2 mL) **baking soda**

¼ tsp (1 mL) **salt**

1. Preheat the oven to 325°F (160°C) and line the bottom of an 8-inch (2-L) square casserole dish with parchment paper.

2. Combine all the ingredients in a bowl and stir until mixed well.

3. Using your fingers, lightly press the mixture into the prepared casserole dish.

4. Bake until lightly browned around the edges and still a bit soft in the middle, about 15 to 20 minutes.

5. Remove from the oven and let cool.

6. Run a knife around the edges of the dish to help free the brownies and turn them out onto a plate.

7. Remove the parchment paper and cut the brownies into squares.

8. Store in an airtight container at room temperature or in the refrigerator. These brownies also freeze well.

HEAVENLY HAZELNUT ICE CREAM

Makes 3 cups (750 mL)

Hazelnuts, or filberts, are—like all nuts—extremely nutritious. They make this rich, creamy dessert high in vitamin E and riboflavin. Hazelnuts are also high in the essential mineral manganese, which is important for normal bone structure development. But most importantly, these nuts taste great! Enjoy this delicious ice cream that is far from "empty calories."

1. Blend the yogurt, hazelnut butter, honey, and vanilla in your food processor or standing blender for a couple of minutes until well-combined and smooth.

2. Pour the yogurt mixture into an ice cream maker and process according to the manufacturer's operating instructions.

3. Transfer to an airtight container and freeze for several hours before serving.

2 cups (500 mL) **YOGURT** (page 27) made from half-and-half (10%) cream

½ cup (125 mL) **hazelnut butter**

½ cup (125 mL) **honey**

2 tsp (10 mL) **PURE VANILLA EXTRACT** (page 36)

CLASSIC VANILLA ICE CREAM

Makes 2½ cups (625 mL)

This dessert staple is perfect on its own, with **WAFFLES AND PANCAKES** (page 61), **RUSTIC PEARS** (page 170), **STRAWBERRY-RHUBARB MINI GALETTES** (page 171), or **GLAZED POUND CAKE** (page 180)—or topped with nuts or fruit.

1. Whisk together the yogurt, honey, and vanilla until thoroughly mixed.

2. Pour the yogurt mixture into an ice cream maker and process according to the manufacturer's operating instructions.

3. Transfer to an airtight container and freeze for several hours before serving.

2 cups (500 mL) **YOGURT** made from half-and-half (10%) cream (page 27)

½ cup (125 mL) **honey**

2 Tbsp (15 mL) **PURE VANILLA EXTRACT** (page 36)

APPLE PIE ICE CREAM

Makes 3 cups (750 mL)

The first thing you might notice about this ice cream is that it's missing a key ingredient—apple. That's because apples are coarse and fibrous, and produce a gritty texture when incorporated into ice cream. Mango, on the other hand, blends smoothly. With its hint of cinnamon, this mango-based dessert tastes all apple.

2 cups (500 mL) **YOGURT** made from half-and-half (10%) cream (page 27)

½ cup (125 mL) **honey**

2 Tbsp (30 mL) **PURE VANILLA EXTRACT** (page 36)

¼ tsp (1 mL) ground **cinnamon**

flesh of 1 ripe **mango**, chopped

1. Purée all of the ingredients in your food processor or standing blender.

2. Pour the yogurt mixture into an ice cream maker and process according to the manufacturer's operating instructions.

3. Transfer to an airtight container and freeze for several hours before serving.

PITTING CHERRIES

Pitting fresh cherries is simple. You can use a cherry or olive pitting tool, or cut the cherries in half and pop out the pit using a small spoon or knife.

CHERRY ALMOND CARAMEL SWIRL ICE CREAM

Makes 3 cups (750 mL)

I invented this decadent dessert for my friend Jane's birthday dinner because she loves cherries. Cherries also happen to be rich in potassium, vitamins C and B, and antioxidants. This ice cream is best made in the summer when cherries are in season, or freeze pitted cherries in the summer and make this ice cream later in the year. —JL

CARAMEL SWIRL

1. Place all the ingredients in a small pot and bring to a boil on high heat.

2. Let boil for 1 to 2 minutes and then remove from the heat.

3. Set aside and let cool to room temperature while you make the ice cream.

¼ cup (60 mL) **honey**

2 Tbsp (30 mL) **butter**

1 Tbsp (15 mL) **YOGURT** made from half-and-half (10%) cream (page 27)

ICE CREAM

1. Purée the yogurt, honey, cherries, and vanilla in your food processor or standing blender for 2 minutes, until smooth.

2. Pour the yogurt mixture into an ice cream maker and process according to the manufacturer's operating instructions.

3. Keep the ice cream in the drum of the ice cream maker and stir in the almond slivers.

2 cups (500 mL) **YOGURT** (page 27)

½ cup (125 mL) **honey**

½ cup (125 mL) pitted fresh or frozen **cherries** (see **PITTING CHERRIES** on page 192)

1 Tbsp (15 mL) **PURE VANILLA EXTRACT** (page 36)

¼ cup (60 mL) **almond slivers**

ASSEMBLY

1. Working quickly, spoon about one-third of the ice cream into a freezer-safe container and scoop half the caramel swirl (which should be quite thick once cooled) on top of it.

2. Top with another third of the ice cream and the rest of the caramel swirl. Top that layer of caramel with the final third of the ice cream.

3. Freeze for several hours before serving.

THE AVALANCHE
Makes 3 cups (750 mL)

Much like the **PEANUT BUTTER CARAMEL CRISPS** (page 185), this dessert will taste familiar. I was inspired to create it after a stop at Dairy Queen on the way to the cottage with my friends where, once again, I was stuck watching rather than eating. Loaded with chunks of sweet peanut butter and nuggets of crispy toffee, this ice cream dream is quite simply heaven. If you want to save time, omit the toffee or replace it with unsalted peanuts. Eat this ice cream plain or on **WAFFLES AND PANCAKES** (page 61). —JL

PEANUT BUTTER CHUNKS

¼ cup (60 mL) unsweetened, unsalted **peanut butter**

2 Tbsp (30 mL) **honey**

1 Tbsp (15 mL) **butter**, melted

1. Combine all the ingredients in a small bowl and mix well. Set aside.

TOFFEE NUGGETS

½ cup (125 mL) **honey**

½ cup (125 mL) **almond**, **cashew**, or **hazelnut butter**

1 Tbsp (15 mL) **butter**

1. Line a baking sheet with parchment paper.

2. Boil the honey in a medium-sized pot on low to medium-low heat until it reaches 300°F (150°C) on a candy thermometer, about 6 to 8 minutes. The honey should boil as vigorously as it can without boiling over. Stir the honey as it boils.

3. Turn off the heat, but keep the pot on the burner. Add the rest of the ingredients and mix well.

4. Pour the hot candy onto the prepared baking sheet.

5. Spread the candy until it is ¼ inch (5 mm) thick. You can do this by placing parchment paper on top of the hot candy and flattening it with a rolling pin or an oven mitt.

6. Chill in the refrigerator until the candy is hard, about 1 hour.

7. Break the hard candy into bite-sized chunks.

ASSEMBLY

1. Make **CLASSIC VANILLA ICE CREAM** (page 191), but whisk in the peanut butter chunks while the ice cream is still in the drum of the ice cream maker. I recommend using a plastic whisk to avoid damaging the drum. If you don't have one, use a metal whisk but be careful not to scrape the inside of the ice cream drum. The peanut butter should form tiny chunks or balls as you whisk.

2. Stir in ¾ cup (175 mL) of the toffee nuggets.

3. Transfer the ice cream to an airtight container and freeze.

MENU PLANNING

In this section of the book you will find all the tools you need for menu planning. We help you create every kind of meal—from simple dinners to lavish entertaining. Just use our meal planning charts, which make it easy to mix and match food ideas. We also spice up mealtime with a guide to breakfast foods that make great lunches, side dishes that work well for breakfast, and lunch soups that are perfect for dinner. Our suggestions will help you try new combinations you just might not have considered.

MEAL PLANNING CHART: ENTERTAINING AT BREAKFAST AND BRUNCH

Planning your breakfast or brunch menu for guests is easy with the following chart, which helps you mix and match dishes beautifully. Below we provide you with some examples that show how to use the chart to create breakfast and brunch meals, but we trust that you will also use your imagination to create your own delicious combinations.

BREAKFAST AND BRUNCH SUGGESTIONS USING THE MEAL PLANNING CHART

HEARTY COTTAGE BREAKFAST

COLUMN A–Fruit Smoothies (pages 69 to 70)

COLUMN A–Waffles (page 61) served with
   berries and

COLUMN E–Simple Syrup (page 37)

COLUMN C–Cheddar Cheese Biscuits (page 57)
   served with

COLUMN E–Orange-Cranberry Marmalade
   (page 39)

ELEGANT BRUNCH

COLUMN A–Fruit Smoothies (pages 69 to 70)

COLUMN A–Crêpes with Brie Cheese and
   Caramelized Apple (page 63) served with

COLUMN E–Simple Syrup (page 37)

COLUMN B–Frittata (page 66)

COLUMN C–Cheddar Cheese Biscuits (page 57)
   served with

COLUMN E–Orange-Cranberry Marmalade
   (page 39)

COLUMN D–Lemon-Cranberry Muffins (page 52)

COLUMN F–Baby Spinach with Goat Cheese
   and Warmed Citrus Vinaigrette (page 112)

A—SMOOTHIES AND SWEET DISHES

Fruit Smoothies (pages 69 to 70)

Pancakes (page 61)

Waffles (page 61) served with berries

Crêpes with Brie Cheese and Caramelized
   Apple (page 63)

Crêpes with Sautéed Pears
   and Raisins (page 64)

Eggnog Omelet or Scramble (page 67)

Warm Crêpes with Jam à la Mode
   (page 168)

Warmed Fruit Omelet (page 67)

Cottage Cheese with Fruit and Candied
   Pecans (page 59)

B—SAVORY DISHES

Vegetable Quiche (page 79)

Ham and Swiss Crêpes (page 65)

Pizza Omelet or Scramble (page 67)

Frittata (page 66)

Gourmet Omelet or Scramble (page 67)

Sunrise Omelet or Scramble (page 67)

Goat Cheese and Caramelized
   Onion Tart (page 105)

continued on next page

C — SAVORY BAKED GOODS

Basic Biscuits (page 56)

Cheddar Cheese Biscuits (page 57)

Dijon Buns (page 123)

D — SWEET BAKED GOODS

Lemon-Cranberry Muffins (page 52)

Muffin-Mix Muffins (page 53)

Carrot and Apple Kugel (page 124)

Sweet Morning Popovers (page 55)

E—JAMS AND SYRUPS

Raspberry Jam (page 40)

Orange-Cranberry Marmalade (page 39)

Simple Syrup (page 37)

Lemon or Orange Syrup (page 37)

Fruit Syrup (page 38)

F—SALADS

Caesar Salad with Ginger Aioli Vinaigrette (page 89)

Romaine Lettuce with "English" French Salad Dressing (page 90)

Mandarin Salad with Citrus Vinaigrette (page 91)

Salad with Toasted Pine Nuts, Goat Cheese, and Apple Cider Vinaigrette (page 92)

Avocado Waldorf Salad (page 93)

Baby Spinach with Goat Cheese and Warmed Citrus Vinaigrette (page 112)

Warm Pecan-Crusted Goat Cheese on Organic Greens (page 111)

MEAL PLANNING CHART: DINNER IS SERVED

This chart will help you plan dinner. Below we have provided you with meal suggestions that illustrate how to use the chart to create a perfect weekday dinner for you or your family, or a special dinner for company. You can also create your own meal combinations by simply going down the columns and choosing what you think you are going to need to fill plates and tummies. Try an Italian-themed dinner or a fondue feast—or one night make the third item in each column. We hope you'll take our suggestion to simply mix and match and try new things.

DINNER SUGGESTIONS USING THE MEAL PLANNING CHART

JODI'S MONDAY NIGHT HOCKEY FAMILY DINNER
COLUMN B–Simple Salad (page 132)
COLUMN E–Steak with Dry-Rub Steak Spice (page 165)
COLUMN D–Five Mushroom Bake (page 120)
COLUMN G–Peanut Butter Ice Box Truffles (page 184)

JODI'S FAVORITE DINNER FOR COMPANY
COLUMN A–Gourmet Pizza with Poached Pear, Caramelized Onion, and Gorgonzola Cheese (page 108)
COLUMN E–Dry-Rub Salmon Barbecued on a Cedar Plank (page 142) served with
COLUMN D–Mango Salsa (page 128)
COLUMN C–Baked Cauliflower (page 131)
COLUMN F–Lemon Freeze (page 175)

JENNY'S FAVORITE DINNER FOR ONE
COLUMN D–Basic Biscuits (page 56)
COLUMN E–"Spaghetti" and Meatballs (page 162)
COLUMN H–The Avalanche (page 194)

JENNY'S FAVORITE DINNER FOR COMPANY
COLUMN B–Avocado Waldorf Salad (page 93)
COLUMN D–Mushroom "Risotto" (page 117)
COLUMN E–Chicken Alfredo (page 153)
COLUMN F–Tiramisu (page 181)

CHEF ROBYN GOOREVITCH'S DINNER FOR TWO
COLUMN C–Steamed Green Beans (page 130)
COLUMN D–Baked Hubbard Squash with Honey and Cinnamon (page 126)
COLUMN D–Caramelized Onion and Celery Root Mash (page 115)
COLUMN E–Rosemary and Mint Rack of Lamb (page 160)
COLUMN F–Grilled Peaches with Sweetened Yogurt Cheese (page 169)

A — STARTERS

Sun-Dried Tomato and Basil Crackers (page 97) served with Goat Cheese (page 31) and Orange-Cranberry Marmalade (page 39)

Baked Brie (page 101) served with apple and pear slices and with Sun-Dried Tomato and Basil Crackers (page 97)

Cheese Fondue (page 102) served with raw vegetables for dipping

Chopped Liver (page 103) served with Sun-Dried Tomato and Basil Crackers (page 97)

Spinach and Cheese Triangles (page 107)

Gourmet Pizza with Poached Pear, Caramelized Onion, and Gorgonzola Cheese (page 108)

Goat Cheese and Caramelized Onion Tart (page 105)

B — SALADS

Simple Salad (page 132)

Caesar Salad with Ginger Aioli Vinaigrette (page 89)

Romaine Lettuce with "English" French Salad Dressing (page 90)

Mandarin Salad with Citrus Vinaigrette (page 91)

Salad with Toasted Pine Nuts, Goat Cheese, and Apple Cider Vinaigrette (page 92)

Avocado Waldorf Salad (page 93)

Baby Spinach with Goat Cheese and Warmed Citrus Vinaigrette (page 112)

Warm Pecan-Crusted Goat Cheese on Organic Greens (page 111)

continued on next page

continued on next page

DESSERT FOR BREAKFAST AND BREAKING OTHER MEALTIME BARRIERS

This section provides lists of dishes that have been recategorized because they work well as meals other than the ones for which they were originally intended: breakfast for dinner, dessert for breakfast, lunch for dinner, and dinner for lunch. But if the idea of eating dessert for breakfast seems odd to you, just remember that **STRAWBERRY-RHUBARB MINI GALETTES** are really just fruit and nuts … a perfect way to start your day!

JENNY'S FAVORITE ALTERNATIVE BREAKFASTS

Cashew Butter Cookies (page 187)
Glazed Pound Cake (page 180)
Sun-Dried Tomato and Basil Crackers with Cream Cheese (page 97)

JODI'S FAVORITE ALTERNATIVE LUNCHES

Goat Cheese and Caramelized Onion Tart (page 105)
Thai Mango Salad (page 113)
Cottage Cheese with Fruit and Candied Pecans (page 59)

JENNY'S FAVORITE ALTERNATIVE DINNERS

Frittata (page 66)
Tuna Melt (page 78)
Carrot Soup (page 82)

JODI'S FAVORITE ALTERNATIVE DESSERTS

Waffles (page 61) with any ice cream (pages 189 to 194)
Crêpes with Sauteed Pears and Raisins (page 64)

BREAKFASTS

Carrot and Apple Kugel (page 124)

Sweet Squash Kugel (page 125)

Spinach and Cheese Triangles (page 107)

Mango Salsa (page 128)

Pineapple Marmalade (page 129)

Thai Mango Salad (page 113)

Apple Cake (page 173)

Strawberry-Rhubarb Mini Galettes
(page 171)

Grilled Peaches with Sweetened Yogurt
Cheese (page 169)

Warmed Crêpes with Jam à la Mode
(page 168)

Egg Salad (page 81)

Sun-Dried Tomato or Basil Crackers (page
97) served with Cream Cheese (see
Cream Cheese on page 28)

Glazed Pound Cake (page 180)

Ginger Cookies (page 186)

Cashew Butter Cookies (page 187)

Cashew Butter Brownies (page 188)

LUNCHES

Waffles or Pancakes (page 61) served with
fruit

Frittata (page 66)

Cheddar Cheese Biscuits (page 57) served
with sandwich fillings (pages 75 to 77)

Spinach and Cheese Triangles (page 107)

Sun-Dried Tomato and Basil Crackers (page
97) served with Chopped Liver (page 103)

Gourmet Pizza with Poached Pear,
Caramelized Onion, and Gorgonzola Cheese
(page 108)

Thai Mango Salad (page 113)

Cabbage Rolls (page 154)

Warm Pecan-Crusted Goat Cheese on
Organic Greens (page 111)

Baby Spinach with Goat Cheese and
Warmed Citrus Vinaigrette (page 112)

Goat Cheese and Caramelized Onion Tart
(page 105)

Cottage Cheese with Fruit and Candied
Pecans (page 59)

DINNERS

Frittata (page 66)

Ham and Swiss Crêpes (page 65)

Tuna Melt (page 78)

Red Lentil Soup (page 86)

Split Pea Soup with Flanken (page 88)

Tomato Soup (page 83)

Carrot Soup (page 82)

Green Vegetable Soup with Chicken (page 85)

Roasted Squash and Apple Soup (page 84)

Any salad (pages 89 to 93) topped with Dry-Rub Salmon Barbecued on a Cedar Plank (page 142) or with steak or chicken with Dry-Rub Steak Spice (page 165)

Cheese Fondue (page 102)

Goat Cheese and Caramelized Onion Tart (page 105)

Basic Crêpes (page 48) and Sandwich Wrap Variations (pages 75 to 77)

DESSERTS

Any of the sweet breakfast crêpes, including Crêpes with Brie Cheese and Caramelized Apple (page 63) and Crêpes with Sautéed Pears and Raisins (page 64)

Waffles (page 61) served with any ice cream (pages 189 to 194)

Fruit Smoothies (pages 69 to 70)

Carrot and Apple Kugel (page 124)

Sweet Squash Kugel (page 125)

Lemon-Cranberry Muffins (page 52)

RESOURCES

WHERE TO BUY ALMOND FLOUR

Many of the recipes in the Grain-Free Gourmet cookbooks use ground almonds or almond flour. Almond flour is often available in bulk-food stores, health-food stores, or the bulk or baking sections of your local grocery store. If you live in Canada or the United States, you can also order almond flour in bulk:

Grain-Free JK Gourmet

www.jkgourmet.com

Telephone 416-782-0045

VIRTUALLY LACTOSE-FREE CHEESES

ASIAGO

BLUE

BRICK

BRIE

CAMEMBERT

CHEDDAR (mild, medium, old, and extra old—note that some people may react to the bacterial culture used to make extra old cheddar cheese)

COLBY

DRY-CURD COTTAGE CHEESE or pressed dry cottage cheese (uncreamed)

EDAM

GORGONZOLA

GOUDA

GRUYÈRE (unprocessed)

HAVARTI

JARLSBERG

LIMBURGER

MONTEREY (Jack)

MUENSTER

PARMESAN (use Italian Parmesan because American Parmesan may have additives)

PORT DU SALUT

PROVOLONE

ROMANO

ROQUEFORT

STILTON

SWISS EMMENTHAL

WEBSITES

INFORMATION ABOUT THE SPECIFIC CARBOHYDRATE DIET AND ITS SUPPORTERS

Breaking the Vicious Cycle
www.breakingtheviciouscycle.info

Grain-Free Gourmet Online
www.grainfreegourmet.com

Grain-Free JK Gourmet
www.jkgourmet.com

Kids & SCD www.pecanbread.com

SCD Web Library www.scdiet.org

Ste. Anne's Country Inn and Spa
www.steannes.com

The Gottschall Autism Center
www.gottschallcenter.com

MEDICAL AND NUTRITIONAL INFORMATION

2005 Dietary Guidelines for Americans
www.cnpp.usda.gov/DietaryGuidelines.htm

Canada's Food Guide to Healthy Eating
www.hc-sc.gc.ca/fn-an/food-guide-aliment/
index_e.html

Dietitians of Canada www.dietitians.ca

Beth Golden, CNP, RNCP
bethgolden1@sympatico.ca

Food and Drug Administration www.fda.gov

Health Canada www.hc-sc.gc.ca

MedlinePlus www.medlineplus.gov

National Osteoporosis Foundation www.nof.org

Osteoporosis Society of Canada
www.osteoporosis.ca

The Mayo Clinic www.mayoclinic.com

WebMD www.webmd.com

FOOD INFORMATION

Almond Board of California
www.almondsarein.com

Amadeus Vanilla Beans
www.amadeusvanillabeans.com

Beef Information Center www.beefinfo.org

CulturAid dairy-free yogurt starter
www.protherainc.com

ProGurt dairy-free yogurt starter
www.progurt.com

Wisconsin Dairy www.wisdairy.com

DHA/EPA Omega-3 Institute
www.dhaomega3.org

BOOKS

Gottschall E. *Breaking the Vicious Cycle: Intestinal Health Through Diet*. Ontario: The Kirkton Press, 2000.

Haas SV and Haas MP. *Management of Celiac Disease*. Philadelphia: J.B. Lippincott Company, 1951.

SELECTED ARTICLES

Abdulkarim AS, Burgart LJ, See J, Murray JA. Etiology of nonresponsive celiac disease: results of a systematic approach. *The American Journal of Gastroenterology* 2002;97:2016–2021.

Amarasiri WA and Dissanayake AS. Coconut fats. *Ceylon Medical Journal* 2006;51(2):47–51.

Anderson CM, Frazer AC, French JM, et al. Coeliac disease: gastro-intestinal studies and the effect of dietary wheat flour. *The Lancet* 1952;1:836–842.

Bibiloni R, Fedorak RN, Tannock GW, et al. VSL#3 probiotic-mixture induces remission in patients with active ulcerative colitis. *The American Journal of Gastroenterology* 2005;100:1539–1546.

Elder JH, Shankar M, Shuster J, et al. The gluten-free, casein-free diet in autism: results of a preliminary double blind clinical trial. *Journal of Autism and Developmental Disorders* 2006;36(3):413–420.

Freund-Levi Y, Eriksdotter-Jönhagen M, Cederholm T, et al. Omega-3 fatty acid treatment in 174 patients with mild to moderate Alzheimer disease: OmegAD study: a randomized double-blind trial. *Archives of Neurology* 2006;63(10):1402–1408.

Fridge J, Kerner J, Cox K. The Specific Carbohydrate Diet—a treatment for Crohn's disease? *Journal of Pediatric Gastroenterology and Nutrition* 2004;39 (Suppl 1): S299–S300.

Garrett WS, Lord GM, Punit S, et al. Communicable ulcerative colitis by T-bet deficiency in the innate immune system. *Cell* 2007;131(1):33–45.

Ghoshal UC, Ghoshal U, Misra A, Chouhuri G. Partially responsive celiac disease resulting from small intestinal bacterial overgrowth and lactose intolerance. *BMC Gastroenterology* 2004;4:10.

Haas SV. Celiac disease and its ultimate prognosis. *The Journal of Pediatrics* 1938;13:390–399.

Haas SV. Celiac disease. *New York State Journal of Medicine* 1963;63:1346–1350.

Haas SV and Haas MP. Diagnosis and treatment of celiac disease: report of 603 cases. *Postgraduate Medicine* 1950; 7:239–250.

Haas SV and Haas MP. The treatment of celiac disease with the specific carbohydrate diet: report on 191 additional cases. *The American Journal of Gastroenterology* 1955;23:344–360.

Helland IB, Smith L, Saarem K, et al. Maternal supplementation with very-long-chain n-3 fatty acids during pregnancy and lactation augments children's IQ at

4 years of age. *Pediatrics* 2003;111(1): e39–44.

Hibbeln JR, Davis JM, Steer C, et al. Maternal seafood consumption in pregnancy and neurodevelopmental outcomes in childhood (ALSPAC study): an observational cohort study. *The Lancet* 2007;369 (9561):578–585.

Jenkins DJ, Kendall CW, Marchie A, et al. Dose response of almonds on coronary heart disease risk factors: blood lipids, oxidized low-density lipoproteins, lipoprotein(a), homocysteine, and pulmonary nitric oxide: a randomized, controlled, crossover trial. *Circulation* 2002;106:1327–1332.

Judge MP, Harel O, Lammi-Keefe CJ. A docosahexaenoic acid-functional food during pregnancy benefits infant visual acuity at four but not six months of age. *Lipids* 2007;42(2):117–122.

Kajander K and Korpela R. Clinical studies on alleviating the symptoms of irritable bowel syndrome. *Asia Pacific Journal of Clinical Nutrition*. 2006;15:576–580.

Nemets H, Nemets B, Apter A, et al. Omega-3 treatment of childhood depression: a controlled, double-blind pilot study. *American Journal of Psychiatry* 2006;163(6):1098–1100.

Nieves R and Jackson RT. Specific Carbohydrate Diet in treatment of inflammatory bowel disease. *Tennessee Medicine* 2004;97(9):407.

Tursi A, Brandimarte G, Giorgetti G. High prevalence of small intestinal bacterial overgrowth in celiac patients with persistence of gastrointestinal symptoms after gluten withdrawal. *The American Journal of Gastroenterology* 2003;98: 839–843.

Wien MA, Sabate JM, Ikle DN, et al. Almonds vs complex carbohydrates in a weight reduction program. *International Journal of Obesity and Related Metabolic Disorders* 2003;27(11):1365–1372.

Whorwell PJ, Altringer L, Morel J, et al. Efficacy of an encapsulated probiotic *Bifidobacterium infantis* 35624 in women with irritable bowel syndrome. *The American Journal of Gastroenterology* 2006;10:1581–1590.

Zemel MB, Thompson W, Milstead A, et al. Calcium and dairy acceleration of weight and fat loss during energy restriction in obese adults. *Obesity Research* 2004;12:582–590.

INDEX

Here's what readers are saying about the first bestselling book in the Grain-Free Gourmet series, *Grain-Free Gourmet: Delicious Recipes for Healthy Living.*

"Those of us who love to cook know that many of the cookbooks we buy are often thumbed through and left on the shelf—this will not be one of those."

"I want to thank you for your amazing cookbook. It has changed my life. Not only can I eat delicious foods, but the change in my diet has been seamless."

"Thank you again so much for your cookbook...I appreciated the cooking tips and the information you included in the book as well. It is more than just a cookbook."

"I just wanted to say thank you for your research and this book. Although I do not have as many of the digestion problems many are battling with, this book has helped me a great deal. I love to cook and also live an all-natural, organic lifestyle, so not only has this cookbook helped me think of baking in a different way, it also accommodates my lifestyle. Thank you for all your hard work— it has been a true blessing for me."

"It's hard to describe what a gift this is. For so many years I have struggled on limited diets to deal with various gut problems. Now I look forward to eating—I know what to eat, feel satiated, and have been able to give up a lifelong and unhealthy chocolate addiction!... I hope you come out with another book some time! I appreciate the good information at the beginning of the book as well. My husband has been a difficult fellow to please food wise, and he loves this food, so we are a happier couple!"

DELICIOUS RECIPES *for* HEALTHY LIVING

grain-free
GOURMET

JODI BAGER *and* JENNY LASS

GRAIN-FREE · REFINED-SUGAR-FREE · LOW-LACTOSE

ISBN 978-1-55285-918-6

"This is absolutely the best cookbook I've ever had. I have been on Specific Carbohydrate Diet for one year and I have a husband and four children. For the past two weeks I have been making recipes from your book and everyone loves all of the recipes. They are delicious and easy to prepare. Now I can make one meal each night and know that they are healthy and delicious and everyone is happy. Thank you for making my life so much easier."